WHEN I LOST MY SON TO HIM

A STORY OF LOVE, GRIEF, AND RESTORATION

CORINE E. PHILLIPS

Paperback: 979-8-218-97117-5

E-Book: 979-8-218-97118-2

Learn more about Corine

Personal Instagram: https://www.instagram.com/mrs_corine/

Business Instagram: https://www.instagram.com/corinephillipsinteriors/

Business Website: https://corinephillips.com/

First Edition

To Michael, my favorite human being.

God promised me that one day, you and
I will serve Him together. Until that day, I
will keep believing and holding on firm to
that promise. I love you.

CONTENTS

1

INTRODUCTION

The first time I wrote half a book, I was about 12 years old. It was a criminal investigation book. Back then, those were the books I particularly enjoyed. After that chapter, it didn't cross my mind that one day, perhaps, I'll be called to write a book, even though for more than a decade, journaling has been a religious practice for me.

Towards the end of 2018, I started embracing the idea of writing an encouraging book for Christian women married to unbelieving men. This idea stemmed from my own experiences, as I was going through the same situation at that time. However, I never completed it due to an unforeseen tragedy that struck my family.

On March 11, 2019, my only son and child, Caleb Toby Phillips, passed away at one of our Methodist hospitals in Houston. I am grateful to the team that tried their utmost to revive him. Caleb was rushed there from the urgent care where he was supposed to receive quick medical help.

In the months that followed Caleb passing away, we went through the fire. In those moments, God not only carried me through it, but He revealed to me the reason behind this event. "The price was too high," I cried out to Him one afternoon. Yes, it was, but with God, I have come to understand that His reckless love for us is as wild as we can imagine.

I come from a culture where death is rarely considered natural. People always assume that if you die, something mystical or someone must have 'dealt with you'. In the couple of days that followed Caleb's departure, I thought I was being punished by God. Had you observed my walk with Christ at that moment in my life, surely, you would have known that my thoughts weren't in alignment with my reality. Why, then, did it happen? I couldn't help but wonder.

When the Lord told me to write this book, I was very reluctant. I feared people might think I was seeking pity. Sharing God's plan behind Caleb's departure made me uncomfortable. I dreaded being viewed as crazy – don't worry, I've made peace with myself about this. I'm okay with you calling me crazy. If I must be, for the sake of my savior, Jesus, then let it be – even by people who knew me. I didn't feel qualified to write and have my book published one day. "When I Lost My Son To Him" is an authentic story of love. It is the story of how I came back home to Christ, of who God became to me, and how the Holy Spirit walked me through the fire unharmed.

When Jesus said in Matthew 11:30 that His yoke is easy and His burden light, I believed it! Though being a believer can be very difficult and depressing at times, it is the willingness to let Him have His way in our lives that allows us to experience the peace that surpasses understanding amid trials.

From the moment Caleb was formed in my womb, God had a plan and a purpose for him. My prayer today is for lives to be transformed by the words in this book. May you see God on every single page. May you experience the peace I experienced amid grief. May you not only cry with me but rejoice as well. I hope that this book will ignite in you the desire to start your authentic walk with Jesus.

2
CHAPTERS

CALEB, OUR HAPPY KID

This little light of mine,

I'm gonna let it shine.

This little light of mine,

I'm gonna let it shine

This little light of mine,

I'm gonna let it shine.

Let it shine, let it shine, let it shine.

Let It Shine – Listener Kids

For this child, I prayed earnestly. He was the only hope I had at that moment to one day believe I could become a mom. I knew I didn't deserve it, but I was determined not to give up until God answered my prayer.

Caleb was born on June 27, 2016, three days after his due date. While he was feeling comfortable in my womb, I couldn't wait to see him. For nine months, I had imagined what he would look like, and I couldn't wait any longer. On his due date, June 24, 2016, my baby sister, Love, and I walked all around Bonapriso in Douala, Cameroon – my neighborhood at the time – hoping it would induce labor. Nothing happened that evening, and we went back home, exhausted. So, on Sunday, I told my boyfriend, Michael, that on his way to work on Monday, we should stop at the hospital because I couldn't wait any longer to see my baby. I called my gynecologist to let him know, and my delivery was scheduled.

Monday morning, around 7:40 AM, I lay in the labor room, and my induction process started. Michael stayed with me for about thirty minutes, then left for work, letting me know he'd be back during his lunchtime. I called my mom to come over, but she was too exhausted because my younger brother Dany and his girlfriend Yanelle, now his wife, had their first child during the night. It was a girl, Oria. Unfortunately, she passed away that same week. She was a premature baby, and she didn't survive. So, my mom promised to be there by the end of the day once she was well rested. According to her, because it was my first delivery, labor would take all day. Then, I called my elder brother, Patrick, in Australia for some prayers and encouraging words. Once I hung up, I took one last selfie of myself, put my phone to the side, and didn't touch it till after labor.

At lunchtime, Michael came back to check on me, and around 1:40 PM, I gave birth to a healthy and big baby boy. "It's a baby! It's a baby!" I said in shock when the midwife handed me Caleb, coming straight out of my womb. I couldn't believe a human being could produce another human being. This made me realize the beauty of this miracle called "delivery". He weighed 3.7 kgs (8.15 lbs). Thank God, I had a relatively fast and safe delivery.

Once delivery was done, Michael, our son, Caleb, and I were

moved to my private bedroom. While I was having lunch, my Aunt Lydie, my mom's elder sister, came in. She couldn't believe what she saw. To her greatest surprise, my labor and delivery went by fast. I stayed four days at the hospital. Every morning, Michael would stop and say hi, and every evening after work, as well. During my entire stay at the hospital, my aunt Lydie was with Caleb and me, taking care of us. She bathed me when I was too weak to do so. She'd watch over Caleb while I'd manage to take a nap. She'd encourage me to breastfeed despite the horrible headache I had – that was the side effect of the epidural I got. Because Caleb was such a big baby, I got a vaginal tear, making it tough on me. I had so many visits from friends and family at the hospital. On my final day there, my parents picked me up, and we went to their house. We had such a warm welcome, with the nursery all set up for us. I stayed there for a month, where Caleb and I were taken care of by my family. Every day at lunch, Michael will come and visit us at my parents' house. According to the company he worked for at that time, he wasn't allowed to visit us at night; it was prohibited. We were living in one of the company's housing units in Bonapriso. During the weekend, we'd go and spend Saturday afternoons with him and go back to my parents' house. After that month at my parents' house, Michael came to pick us up, and we went back to our house.

God heard my cry. I was now a mom, for real.

When Caleb was a baby, I used to spend hours staring at him while he was sleeping. I'd take breaks in between to do some other stuff, but I'd always come back to just look at my son sleeping in his crib. I couldn't believe something so perfect came out of me, the imperfect. Michael used to love laying Caleb on his chest and letting him sleep. One night, he went into Caleb's bedroom and let him sleep on his chest, and he, too, fell asleep. At some point during the night, I heard my baby cry so loud that it woke me up. I went to his room just to see him lying on the floor, screaming. He fell off Michael's chest. Thankfully, he landed on the high pile rug by the bed. I got so upset that night with Michael. And in my mama bear anger, I remembered hitting him so hard because he hurt my baby. He didn't wake up because he was too tired and perhaps drunk to do so. I took my baby and brought him into my room. He was only two months old. Even though that made me so mad, I did recognize later on that behind that incident was a dad madly in love with his son. Caleb was everything to Michael. For him, he could kill. He one day told me He never thought he'd bear a child of his own. His ex-wife never bore him kids, so, at some point in his life, he lost hope of being a biological dad. Caleb was his miracle.

Back in my university years, I had a good friend from my youth church whose name was Caleb. Before him, I had never heard that name. I thought it was a cute and unique name. So, I told Corine, my best friend from university, that one day, if I have a boy, I'll call him Caleb.

Six years later, I was expecting a boy, and I knew what his name would be. So, one night, I told Michael I wanted our son to be called Caleb. Michael used to be very discreet about his life at the beginning of our relationship. He never talked about his family in the US. When I asked, he would hardly answer - I wasn't sure whether he had things to hide or he didn't trust me enough yet to share family information with me. Perhaps it was a little bit of both. He said he'll think about it. About a week or two later, he came back and told me he had found a name for our son, and it would be, wait for it, Caleb! And right when I was about to say, "Wait a minute, isn't that what I suggested?" he told me that was his deceased brother's name and he'd love for our son to be named after him. There was nothing I could add to that. History would remember that our son was meant to be called Caleb because his mommy loved that name, and his daddy wanted to honor the memory of his deceased brother by naming his son after him.

Hiring a nanny in Cameroon is something relatively easy and common. We had one for Caleb, and this allowed us, especially me, to breathe. This is something I've always loved about my country – it takes a village to raise a child. Whether it's free or not, the 'village' is always there. You hardly ever feel lonely. Help of some kind is almost always available. I came to appreciate it more when we moved to the US because now I was a full-time mom, and in 18 months of Caleb's age, I had not experienced the fullness of solely taking care of my child. In a way, that made me more present and closer to my son. Everywhere I went, he'd be with me. At some point, I called him my mini-me because I saw myself in him. He was such a loving and gentle boy.

One afternoon – he was about two years old – he and I were at the dining table having lunch, and Michael was taking a nap on the sofa. When Caleb finished his plate, he got down and went towards his dad. He looked at me, pointed at his dad, and said, "ee sheepy," meaning, "he's sleeping". I shook my head in agreement and told him not to wake his dad up. So he went into his bedroom, got his teddy bear, placed it inside Michael's arms, and kissed his dad on the forehead. I could not believe what I saw. How and when did my son see this? I used to put Caleb's teddy bear in his arms when he was taking a nap, and I used to give Michael kisses on his forehead almost every single time I saw him sleeping in our bed. I had no idea when or how my son observed me do these things. To see him do that gave me a huge smile and a sense of pride. I was raising a gentle and loving boy, and what I did, he was copying. I think from that day forward, I became most cautious about the way I behaved in his presence.

There's another time when he made me laugh hard. I used to move things around our apartment a lot. I was an amateur art lover, and at that time, I was also taking my interior design certificate. So, one night, Michael was out of town, and it was just Caleb and I home. I pulled out my stuff to hang art. So, this is me on the table, adjusting the print in the frame, and here comes Caleb with my panty liner. He took off the adhesive band and stuck the panty liner on the wall, then took two steps back and observed it on the wall, then went back to adjust it and stir at it to make sure "his art" was well hung. My goodness, I couldn't help it. I was dead laughing because this, again, was all me. I did record the entire scene from the moment I saw him with my panty liner. My little finger told me he was up to something, so I made sure to have it on tape. Unfortunately, I lost that video. There was also this other video of him where I caught him in my bathroom putting on my panty liner on his underwear.

Caleb was so silly and fun to be around. Such a happy kid. He was also my cuddle partner. We both had it in common that we loved cuddling, sucking on our tongues, and rubbing on each other like cats do. This is most definitely one of the things I loved and missed the most about Caleb – his cuddles and hugs.

Some of the things I used to love sharing with my son were swimming lessons. He started taking lessons a little before he was two years old. We did the parent-kid lessons, where we'd be in the pool together. By the time he passed away, he had graduated to the next level, where he went into the pool by himself and didn't need mommy anymore. He was making good progress, and I was so proud of him. At the swimming school, they gave him this swimming coin that I still keep with me everywhere I go.

Fashion was something I got him into as well. My son was so handsome and stylish. At the time, I did not realize how gorgeous that little boy was until he passed away. Everywhere he went, he would attract compliments. It made me uncomfortable sometimes because he was a child, but I used to receive a lot of compliments from strangers on how beautiful and stylish I was. I guess dogs don't make cats. Sometimes, he'd stay up with me and play around with me when I was selecting outfits for my Instagram style and fashion account. I shared outfit inspiration. It used to take a lot of outfits trying before filming, and my son used to keep me company. While I was playing around with clothes, he was playing with his toys and sometimes would wear my shoes for fun.

With Caleb by my side, I always thought about ways I could better myself. His presence in my life encouraged me to do more and to follow my dreams. I felt it even more during the time I was going through my Interior design diploma. When I enrolled in that course, I decided to put Caleb at the daycare. It gave me more time during the day to focus on studying. Some nights, I would work late, too, and as long as Michael was around watching over Caleb, I could keep pushing. One week, though, Michael was out of town again for work. I was working on a module that was very difficult for me. We had to create a floor plan using CAD, and that was tough. So, that one night, I decided I wouldn't go to bed until I was done with it. I fed Caleb, gave him his bath, and let him watch TV while I was working. I was so focused that I didn't realize it was getting late. Caleb started doing something in my back, but I didn't care too much to watch. My son was very independent, and on purpose, I used to let him mess up so he could learn a lesson or two. It was nothing too dangerous, though. At some point, it has been silent for a while. My desk was in the kitchen. So, I turned, and I saw my son lying on the floor, sleeping, with pillows all around him and his red blanket. I couldn't help it. I took a picture; then I cried – I'm too emotional sometimes. My son didn't want to disturb me. So, he silently made a bed next to me and let me work, probably thinking I'd take us to bed when I was ready for bed.

When he passed away a couple of months after this, I wasn't done with my diploma and almost gave up because I didn't have the desire to keep going if Caleb wasn't there to stick with me. After all, despite my passion for design, I desired to build a legacy for my son through my passion. I wanted him to be proud of his mom one day when he'd be old enough to say, "My mom is a successful interior designer." Unfortunately, it will never happen that way, and that, till today, breaks my heart.

As our baby boy was growing into a toddler, he started developing new characters of his own. He became assertive and authoritative, especially at home with Michael and I. Outside, he was chill and easygoing most of the time. He wouldn't open up much to strangers but he remained cordial. He was his dad's buddy. Michael will drop him off in the morning at the daycare and pick him up in the evening on his way back home. That was their father-son time. They had their rituals I didn't always know about, and that was fine by me.

At a very young age, Caleb loved God. He'd sing all the Listener Kids songs out loud, and he'd dance to them. I taught my son how to honor God and rejoice in the things of the Lord. I took him to church with me whenever I could. I was determined to give to him what my mom gave us — the fear and love of God. I'm so happy that I was able to carry that challenge for the short time he lived.

One of the anime Caleb got into and which he was so passionate about was PJ Masks. He was obsessed with those guys. He'd sing the entire cartoon generic to the top of his lungs at home. One week before he passed, he gave us a little show at home. I took a video of him because the energy he was releasing was worth filming. The PJ Masks crew was coming to Sugar Land, Texas, for a show, and Michael got us tickets. The weekend we were supposed to go watch it, Caleb got ill. That Sunday morning, we were hesitant to go because he was so weak and lethargic. Nonetheless, we decided to take him to see his favorite anime. The show was amazing. Caleb had fun but not too much because he wasn't feeling good. We got him a t-shirt with his favorite PJ Mask hero — Catboy. That year, three months from that day, Caleb was going to turn 3, and I was planning on throwing him a PJ Mask party. I thought I'd keep the t-shirt till his birthday came. But the next day, when Michael came to pick us up to go to the urgent care, something in my mind thought — today is a great day to wear your best t-shirt. So, I dressed him in his blue PJ Mask t-shirt we bought the day before. Our son passed away that Monday.

Caleb was as unique as his name was. He was genuinely loved by people around him. Strangers found him stylish, and family found him cute. To Michael and me, he was our biggest pride and our source of joy. Not a month nor a year goes by without us wishing we could hug and love on him one last time.

GO TO THE LAND I WILL SHOW YOU

You are the grave where our fathers sleep,

The garden that our ancestors have cultivated.

We work to make you prosperous

One fine day we will finally get there.

Be Africa's faithful child

And always progress in peace

Hoping that your young children

Will love you without bounds forever.

**The Rallying Song (Cameroon's National Anthem)
– René Djam Afame**

It was Monday, January 1st, 2018, that I officially moved to the United States with my boyfriend Michael and our son Caleb, who was one and a half years old at that time. I came to a land that was foreign to me, and honestly, I did not want to be here at all! Michael took Caleb and me here for the first time a little before Thanksgiving 2017 to visit his family. I enjoyed the month we spent between Florida and Louisiana. Visiting was nice, but moving was something I had a hard time dealing with. I loved my life in Cameroon, and I couldn't see myself living elsewhere, especially not in the United States of America.

As I was planning to relocate, I was co-owning an event planning company with my best friend, Ornella. We had been in business for just under a year. Our shared passion and dedication were so strong that we believed firmly in our success. I cherished our sessions bouncing back creative ideas; how I miss those times! The decision to move to the United States was not easy. It meant leaving behind not just my family and friends, but also the business I loved and my life in Cameroon. To truly understand the difficulty of this decision, you need to understand why my love for my country is so deep.

I was born in Yaoundé − our capital − and raised in Douala − our largest city and economic capital − by my dad, who is from the Ewondo tribe, and my mom, who is from the Bafoussam tribe. I'm what you'll consider a city girl, very sheltered and spoiled, especially by my dad at that time. I'm the second of 6 siblings, of whom I grew up with three brothers, Patrick, Cedric, and Dany, in the same house. My sister, Love, and my brother, Brian, ten and fifteen years younger than me, respectively, were too young when I left my parents' house for boarding school and eventually university. So, my childhood memories with these last two are different from those of my three other brothers − the first four of us are closer in age.

One of the things that make Cameroon so unique is its culinary diversity. A friend once told me, "You can live 365 days in Cameroon, and every single day, you get to eat a new meal." Now, I can't account for that, but I can say it's close to the truth because of the 250 tribes that we have, and you bet each tribe has at least one native main dish. My country is known as "Africa in miniature" because of our cultural and geographical diversity. We have beautiful, impenetrable tropical forests full of wild animals like chimpanzees, gorillas, forest elephants, and buffalo, beaches with white and black sand, high mountains and volcanoes, deserts, and so much more. Did I also mention that we have the biggest frogs in the world – Goliath Frogs? There is so much to see about that country. Myself, I haven't explored much of it, simply because our tourism industry isn't as developed. Thankfully, over the past couple of years I've been in the US, I've seen through social media how it is developing at a fast pace.

Some of the things I miss the most about Cameroon while living in the US are the food, the streets I grew up in and lived in with my closest friends, my extended family members – my siblings all live abroad – and my parents. I'm blessed to have lived in a peaceful and safe neighborhood. We were more of a middle-class family, with my dad working in Oil and Gaz and my mom in Insurance. I remember my life to be, for the most part, happy and peaceful. Of course, we had tough times, too, but our parents did a great job of providing the best they could, and for that, I'm more than grateful. Our neighbors were like family. There is a saying in Cameroon that goes, "It takes a village to raise a child." Back home, that saying was literal. We had friends in all the different neighboring blocs. Despite the rain during summer vacation, that time of the year was my favorite. We'd play all types of outdoor games till the sun went down, and summer snacks like grilled corn and plumb, boiled peanuts, and black fruits were enough to make this little girl happy. Life was that simple and enjoyable.

My brothers and I grew up at the Pentecostal church, where my mom used to go to. She was always so intentional about teaching us humility, simplicity, and kindness. There were times as a child when I wondered why my mom, with all the class and chic she had, would be a member of some type of churches. Truth be told, back in those days, Pentecostal churches used to be full of financially poor people. It was as if, at that time, poverty was associated with holiness, and those spiritually revived Christians seemed to me as if they loved their poor life. Things have changed with time, and I thank God that the house of God no longer settles for the cheapest stuff. Being a believer is also being excellent. I'm not talking here about the "prosperity gospel", but it makes no sense to me that the Bible says that to our God belongs all the riches, and we're fine settling in material poverty. However, with time and maturity, I came to strongly appreciate that my mom taught us how to mingle with people from various backgrounds. I loved that she didn't care whether she went to a rich people's church or not. She was happy being around people she had something in common with – Jesus! My dad was Catholic, but it never influenced us because he didn't go to church much, and I always thought he just entrusted my mom with our spiritual upbringing.

My brothers and I went to a private school where we learned both French and English. I can't thank my parents enough, especially my mom, for deciding to send us to a school that, at that time, was probably the only fully bilingual school in our country. My dad once told me it was a very difficult decision to make. Their friends and family didn't understand why they'd choose to burden little children like us with the complete French curriculum and the English curriculum. According to them, that was too much for a child to learn. Even though my dad had a decent job with a very good salary, sometimes it was a stretch for him, but he was psychologically ready to take the challenge. The importance my dad placed on education was high. He would rather starve but send his kids to the best school in town. "Knowledge and education are wealth and freedom", he always said! So, from my nursery school years up to my first year of high school, I went to Horizon Bilingual Educational Complex. After that, I went to boarding school at St Francis College in Kumba to finish my high school years. My experience there taught me a lot about discipline, hard work, and dedication. For three school years, I lived away from home, and my focus was to succeed and bring home good grades my parents – especially my dad – would be proud of. It was during those years that I started developing night owl characters. With my classmates, during exam time, we'd stay up at night to study. It got worse when I went to university. Today, I'm still a late-night worker, and I'm not sure it will ever change. I'd love to be an early bird one day, though.

If there is a time in my life that I wish I could go back to and freeze, it's definitely my university years. That was the best time of my life. For the first time ever, I had my own home. At my parents' house, I never had my own room; I always had to share it with one aunt or one cousin, and sometimes I'd have to sleep in the living room because occasionally my room was turned into a guest's bedroom. But now, I was living in a studio apartment by myself, and I felt free. I had a group of friends with whom I loved hanging out. They were mostly guys, and that's because I was in an Engineering school, which was, at that time, a male-dominated industry. However, I had my very special university bestie, Corine, who today I consider a sister. She truly was the cherry on my university cake life. She taught me how to cook some native meals. We ran a pancake-and-cake-baking business together for some time. She knew me like an open book, from the worst things I have ever done in my life to the good ones. Yet, she didn't love me less. She was a believer, too, and the voice of wisdom in my life at that moment. I truly needed that spiritual guidance from time to time. I didn't do a lot of partying as someone might think. The school was hard enough. What I loved the most was the freedom of being me and expressing myself in a way that I liked and had never done before. I never experienced the worldly life before. I was what people called "a gate child" — the type of child who grew up too sheltered with no knowledge of street life. Now, the world was open to me, and I became curious about it. It was also at that period that I started my fashion blog and partnered with my dearest childhood friend, Nancy, to run an online African accessories shop.

My dream of becoming an interior designer was also birthed when I was in university. I hated engineering school, to be honest. I did it because my dad wanted me to. Being an engineer, a doctor, a lawyer, or an accountant was one of those fields parents took pride in knowing their kids were doing or would one day become. Eventually, I became an Occupational Health and Safety Engineer, which I was very proud of. The idea of caring for people's safety at work as well as their health was something I enjoyed doing. Following my dad's footsteps, he helped me get my first real job at the same Oil & Gaz service company where my boyfriend Michael was working. It started as an internship with a promise of a long-term contract.

Although I didn't work there as long as I was promised to, it was nonetheless an experience that marked my career and my life.

There, I met one of the most amazing ladies in my life, my best friend, Ornella. The story of our friendship is funny because she was originally Michael's best friend at work. I heard about her way before I started working there. He always had so many nice things to say about her that it struck my curiosity. I remember during my first days there, I got her and my direct supervisor small gifts. I thought it would be a nice icebreaker and perhaps a way of saying I'd love to know you better. It didn't take too long for us to become friends. She was the first person Michael and I announced Caleb's pregnancy. She has loved and taken care of Caleb like her own child. At that time, she didn't have a child yet. Today, she has the cutest little girl ever, Zaza. Around Caleb's sixth month, Ornella and I started our event planning business – I've always been an entrepreneur at heart.

Caleb was a little over a year old when Michael told me we would be moving to the US. At that point, relocating to another country wasn't something I envisioned anymore. Traveling overseas was, for me, something I'd do for vacation reasons only, not relocation. After all, when you make decent money back home, you can afford to travel wherever you want in the world. You truly have the best of both worlds. It is true that when I finished high school to go to university, my first choice was to study aviation, my forever dream job, in Canada. I loved that it was as equally bilingual as my country, and what I knew about it pleased me. My dad failed me on that one, and I ended up doing Engineering in Cameroon. That's why my grades were so bad in my first years of university. I was hoping my dad would see how miserable I was not to study aviation and eventually would send me abroad. It didn't work. So, as I grew into this woman in Cameroon, I knew this was my place to make a name for myself, and with Ornella, the journey we started looked promising. When that news came to me, it was a shock! I did not want to go, and I wasn't fond of the US. Yes, I loved American Pop Rock and RNB, but living there was a no-no for me. I've watched too many murder stories on TV with Michael that I believed I'd be kidnapped and killed, and my story will come up on Investigation Discovery. I viewed the US as being a very unsafe place, and I wasn't going to sacrifice myself or my son. Michael could go back; after all, it was his home, not mine. Moreover, I wasn't his wife. I was just his girlfriend, and nothing obliged me – especially because he had sworn never to get married again – to follow him.

When the relocation topic came up, I had reconsecrated my life to Christ, and one thing I promised God was to always seek his perfect will for my life. Though I had all these doubts and fears, I knew I had to go before my father in the secret place and seek his guidance. One afternoon, I told my son's nanny not to knock at my door, no matter what was happening. I wasn't going to get out of my room till God spoke to me. Caleb's nanny used to be my Sunday school teacher at my mom's church when I was a child. She saw me grow, and somehow, I trusted her motherly instincts. She was so good to Caleb, almost like a grandma to him, and she loved him so tenderly. I shared a little bit about my fears with her and how important it was for me to seek God's guidance. For about 3 hours in that bedroom, I prayed and cried for God to speak to me. Back then, I didn't read my Bible as much. I relied a lot on hearing from God in my spirit, and up till then, I was still learning how to recognize God's voice. Towards the end of those hours, I was lying flat on the floor, and I heard "Joshua 1:9". I had no idea what that scripture was nor if I made that up, but I rushed to open my bible, and there it was: *"Have I not commanded you? Be strong and courageous. Do not be afraid; do not be discouraged, for the Lord your God will be with you wherever you go."*

I fervently hoped that God would advise me against going, as I deeply wished not to. Reluctantly facing the prospect of abandoning my life and dreams in Cameroon, I was torn about following a man who had vowed never to marry me. Overwhelmed, I sobbed uncontrollably, my prayers a murmur amidst tears: "Lord, how can I serve you rightly if I am to remain forever a girlfriend, living a life unworthy of my calling? I long to be a wife, honoring the value you place on marriage. I believe you can lead me to a husband who will embrace my son and together, we can serve you. Why then do you ask me to follow someone indifferent to faith and marriage?"

After more tears, as I found calmness, I distinctly heard the Holy Spirit's guidance in my spirit. Realizing the significance of this moment, one of the first times I had heard the Lord so clearly, I knew I must document it. Here is an excerpt from my journal, slightly edited for clarity, yet the essence of the story remains unchanged.

*Do you remember what the writer said in her book? The one you read recently. Some women tend to leave before reaping what they've sowed for months or even years. Why does this happen? This is because they didn't trust God enough to let Him work that miracle for them. They got impatient and left. Don't make this mistake a second time. Years ago, you did it with *****, and you left. I know there have been moments when you regretted that action. You let your emotions take control of your actions. But because I love you, I sent someone else for you, Michael. I see you sowing in his life, and that makes me happy. Your deepest desire is for him to know me, and I like that. Don't ever give up. I know* *you're an impatient woman, but I am a patient God. I will teach you patience, and at the end of this journey, you will be a better woman. I know it's not easy, but I need you to trust me. Like Jesus, I know you'd rather have me take away this cup from you, but remember that good things do not always come easily. Keep praying and asking what exactly you would want to see in your future husband… or should I call him Michael? I am in control.*

Two months later, I moved to Houston with Michael and our son Caleb. Six months after that, on June 2nd 2018, two days before my birthday, we got married.

NO MATTER WHAT, I STILL LOVE YOU

There's no shadow You won't light up
Mountain You won't climb up
Coming after me
There's no wall You won't kick down
Lie You won't tear down
Coming after me

Reckless Love – Cory Asbury

In Cameroon, we have two major seasons – the Dry and the Rainy seasons, unlike in the Western world, where there are four seasons – Winter, Spring, Summer, and Fall (my favorite season). The months that fall under the Summer Season here in the US coincide with the Rainy Season when all the students are on their biggest vacation time. It was during that time that, as a teenager, I gave my life to Christ for the 'first time' at a youth camp organized by my church. It was the Summer of 2007. That same year, I was also admitted to the University of Douala, Cameroon, to study Industrial Engineering.

I don't know of any church in my hometown, Douala, in those days that had a section just for the youth. My church was so cool that our youth ministry was called 'JAD – Jeunesse Avec Difference, meaning Youth With a Difference' in English. We were young, anointed, talented, and full of energy, like an army ready to serve the Lord Jesus with all that we had. We were D.O.P.E.!!! For two full years, I faithfully and consistently served God in our youth ministry before becoming very sporadic and eventually abandoning the house of the Lord for about six years.

Returning from youth camp that summer, my brother Dany and I decided to get baptized. I always admired how he served God - his profound love for people and his desire to see them saved, evident even at a young age. Remarkably, he became a youth leader before I did, showing a deeper commitment to his faith than I initially had.

Eventually, I began bible lessons to also become a youth leader, although I never completed the final class. I joined the translators' team as well, alongside two other passionate and dynamic young women. Our primary role was to translate our youth Pastor's sermons from French to English in real time, and occasionally from English to French.

Elizabeth, the eldest of us, quickly became a close friend. She encouraged and taught me to pray confidently in the spirit. We often spent long hours in prayer, either at my studio apartment at university or at her parent's house. I recall a night at her place when we prayed in the spirit for an hour - a duration I have never reached since, haha.

I enjoyed serving God with my friends in my youth. We were so on fire for Jesus. The type of declarations and prayers we used to make were wild. We would say things like, "Lord, we will preach your Gospel to the ends of this world. We will abandon anything we have to serve you. We will let you use us in any way possible." Some of those prayers are still active in some of our lives. Yes, we were teenagers, and we struggled with the same things teenagers struggle with, but we were different because we had Jesus. It makes sense to me today as an adult that the enemy is so much more after the youth because a young person serving God is like blazing fire you won't know how to stop. My prayer is for my children to serve God at a very young age and never depart from Him. I'm hopeful that my experiences will serve them in their journey with the Lord.

In those days, as new believers, we had spiritual mentorship. I had two spiritual fathers I looked up to. I remembered that at some point, there was this guy at church I fell in love with, and he loved me too. I knew him and his brother since we were pre-teens because that was still the same church we'd been going to all this time. This wasn't the church my mom went to. My brothers and I went to this church with my big cousin because it was closer to our house, in the suburbs. Sometimes, we'd walk to church, and sometimes we'd take a taxi. My mom's church was further away in town, and she didn't have a car back then, so it was expensive for her to pay for a taxi for her four kids – my three brothers and I – and herself. That's how our big cousin suggested we join her church to ease my mom's financial burden. She didn't find any objection because it was still a Pentecostal church.

So, I had never been interested in this guy until then. By that time, I was approaching my twenties. Both my spiritual fathers didn't want me to pursue that relationship because the guy wasn't good for me, and he had the reputation of being a heartbreaker. At least, that's what they said. One thing about me was I didn't like it when someone imposed on me what to do without clearly explaining why. Coming from an African home where elders are usually not questioned, I was that unique type of girl who used to fight back. I used to be stubborn and rebellious. I'm way less today because I've matured and learned my lessons. To be stubborn has its good and bad sides. So, I told them both that I'd pursue the relationship. I've always been very honest with myself and the people around me. Americans don't like that. I've been called "blunt," "rude," "direct," and "matter-of-fact" in the US. In my defense, it is grounded in my Cameroonian education, and I'm fine with that.

One of my spiritual fathers made it a mission to end that relationship. The more he tried, the more I stood firm on my ground. My bad luck was my spiritual father was a neighbor to this guy who now was my boyfriend. Sometimes, when I visit my boyfriend, my spiritual father would see me and make me trouble at church. It reached a point where he started saying funny things about me to the other youth leaders in the church. Someone came to me and told me he said I was seducing him, my spiritual father. Soon enough, I was looked at as a mini-Jezebel. Eventually, because I couldn't stand that atmosphere, I decided to stop attending youth leaders' bible training. I also opted out of translating. Then, one day, I told myself that people in the church, especially leaders who are supposed to know God better, would do these types of things to me; why should I be among them? Perhaps living my life in the world would be better, I thought. I left the church.

In my years away from God, I discovered sex, seduction, and exciting nightlife. My bad behaviors were magnified to the point where I knew I was unworthy to be called a believer, and honestly, I was fine with it. After all, I despised their lies and spiritual sense of control, and I didn't want to be associated with Christians. My boyfriend – not the one from church, I broke up with him – and I both lost our virginities together. For years before that, I took pride in my virginity, and I desired so badly to keep it until I got married one day. I was 23 years old when it happened. For a beautiful young girl like me, I was very late, at least according to the culture. I started living my life on my terms. I wasn't listening to Christian music anymore; if so, it was because the melody was cool but nothing deep. I cut most of my friends from my youth church off, even that boyfriend. Life was fun. At least, that's how it felt, and honestly, I did enjoy it for years, but the truth about living life away from God is the lack of fulfillment and contentment. It's like you're always after the next thrill until you get to a point where you're emotionally and mentally empty and broken. When you hit that point, it's like your life doesn't make sense anymore. You're just doing things because you're still alive; you don't have any other choice. In the worst-case scenario for some people, life becomes so meaningless that they decide to give it an end.

By now, I had been living a life unworthy of my calling in Christ for four years. I was 26 years old, and at the end of summer that year, Nancy introduced me to Michael. I had been single for three months at that time. Believe it or not, ever since I started dating when I was 13 years old, that was the longest time I had ever been single. I didn't know back then that I had a serious fear of being single. All I knew was I had to be in a romantic relationship because, for me, I had all this love I needed to share with a partner. Later, as an adult, I faced this disorder, addressed it, and let the Holy Spirit heal me. With Michael, it wasn't love at first sight, on the contrary. I had heard enough in my history class about the slave trade and European colonization to know that people from his race weren't my friends. But very fast, he won my heart, and I dropped my guard. Unlike the previous relationship I was coming from, Michael loved me just as I was. He never tried to change my style, and more than anything, he loved my braids and would never fail to compliment me. I became so madly in love with him that when he asked me to move in with him, I didn't hesitate. At that time, I had already graduated as a Safety Engineer, and I was studying for a British Safety Certification called NEBOSH.

Shortly after we moved in together, Michael and I became co-workers in an oil and gas service company in my hometown. My dad helped me get a job at that company through a connection he had made in the industry. My dad had been working for a well-renowned oil and gas company in town for more than 20 years now, and his managerial position gave him some leverage. Mike was also a well-established ex-pat worker at our company. Meanwhile, I was in my internship months, with a strong promise of a contract after the internship. It was the arrangement my dad and his connection friend made for me. After about four months of working there, Michael and I got pregnant.

It was 5 a.m., and I was sitting on the toilet in the powder room, waiting for my pregnancy test result to show up. I didn't want to disturb Michael's sleep. That's why I didn't take the pregnancy test in our bathroom. My heart was pounding – what if it was positive? What will I do?

It was on a Saturday morning that I conceived. It was like a joke to me. I wasn't sure that my body was able to create life. Of course, I knew babies were made that way, but my brain was so naïve and immature that I didn't fully believe I could conceive.

The pregnancy test results came out positive. It was surreal. Was I really having life inside me? I never realized I did until after I committed the unthinkable later down the line. I didn't have too much time to think about it that morning. I had to get ready for work. Michael, another coworker, and I were living together in that flat. They were both expat, and I was local.

The week that followed the test result, I started having the symptoms of a pregnant woman. I was tired all the time, fell asleep in the taxi so often, and I even got so dizzy one time at work that one coworker spoke out loud, "I think you're pregnant". Just for my supervisor to say, "We both can't be pregnant." I never admitted to them that I was. I wasn't even sure that I wanted to keep the pregnancy. I was conflicted. I had just started this internship, and I wanted to secure my job. Moreover, I didn't want to be pregnant and unmarried. Yet, I had always wanted to be a mom. It was hard enough to live with my boyfriend and deal with people's opinions, especially from my Christian community. How much more being pregnant out of wedlock? Like Christians used to say back home, I was considered a 'backslider', but still, I didn't want to make my case worse, even though the church wasn't a thing for me anymore.

I turned to Corine, who was the only one I shared the news with. She, too, was on fire for the Lord in our first years of university, and like me, left the church at some point, got pregnant out of wedlock but had her son, and ended up marrying her boyfriend, with whom they had two more kids. Today, like me, she's back in the house of the Lord and for good! So I could identify with her. She told me to keep the pregnancy. And whenever I felt unsure, she would come to visit me and beg me not to give my pregnancy away. Life was more important than a job and public opinion, she said.

By then, Michael and I had moved already to our own apartment. One night, we talked about it, and we seemed to be okay with keeping the pregnancy. In fact, we were excited by it, and he even told his mom. Though I didn't know her by then, I overheard her on the phone, and she seemed pleased to be a grandma. Somehow, my mom's opinion and approval mattered more to me, and I wasn't sure how I was going to tell her or how she'd received the news. I was so scared that the reasons why it would be a bad idea to keep the pregnancy became so magnified to me – we were not married, and I just started work. After a long discussion with Michael, we decided we were not going to keep the pregnancy. His argument was if I kept the pregnancy, I might not receive the contract at the end of my internship. And because working in oil and gas was such a great opportunity for my career and my financial stability, I shouldn't jeopardize my chances. I knew he said it in my best interest, but at the same time, I wasn't sure if I should do it or not. I blamed myself later because I felt like I planted the seed of doubt in him.

One night, Corine returned home, and we revisited the discussion about my pregnancy. She implored me not to terminate it, sharing how difficult her experience had been but ultimately expressing happiness for not doing so. I resolved that evening to discuss it with my mom, deciding that her support would be my deciding factor.

The most daunting aspect for me was the anticipated reaction of my mom, her church friends, and my former church community. My mom, a deaconess, had already struggled to accept my cohabitation with a man outside of marriage. The thought of having a child in these circumstances without the prospect of marriage troubled me deeply.

After Corine left, I phoned my mom to tell her. I secretly hoped she would encourage me to keep the baby. Instead, she cried throughout our conversation, lamenting what she perceived as a departure from the Christian values I was raised with. She worried about the judgment of her friends and the church community. The call ended ambiguously, without any definitive guidance. I didn't disclose my consideration of an abortion. Her tears deeply wounded me, leading me to believe that terminating the pregnancy might restore some normalcy.

I was engulfed in feelings of failure and disappointment towards my mother. At that point, I was oblivious to many aspects of abortion, including the fact that there was already a tiny heartbeat within me. Looking back, I realize that had I fully understood the existence of life inside me, my decision might have been different. I was naive and uninformed, having done no research whatsoever before contemplating such a significant decision.

The first thing I did when I woke up the next day was to get money from Michael, call the clinic, and schedule an appointment with my gynecologist that afternoon. I went to work, and by midday, I got permission to go to the clinic. I was in the taxi, turning at the light close to the clinic, and in the opposite direction, I saw my mom in her car. I thought to myself, "I hope this will fix things."

I got into my gynecologist's office, and I told him I needed to interrupt the pregnancy. I was worried about whether it was going to be painful or not. He reassured me everything would be all right. He took my money, placed it inside his drawers, and asked me to lie on the bed where I usually lay during my consultation. He was always so kind, gentle, and reassuring. That afternoon as well. Then he started the procedure. It was painful. By the time he was done, I thought internally "I should have never done this". It was too late. I just had an abortion. My heart was screaming, "Please put it back inside me". But there was no turning back. I sat on the chair opposite him, physically drained and dizzy, and I whispered, "I'm weak; I feel like I'm dying." This was the first and only time in my life I fell death so close. It felt like my spirit was about to leave my body. He held my hand and said I should take the afternoon off and rest, which I did.

Later that evening, my mom called me when I was home.

"Allo?"

"Yes, Mom."

"We're going to keep it ok. It's not a big deal. We will keep it."

"Mom, it's not there anymore; the doctor took it out this afternoon."

"Oh, my Jesus! What have you done, Corine? Why Lord? Why?" My mom screamed that evening and burst into tears. We were both crying. I was confused. I was disgusted. I was aggravated, and more than everything, I was so broken that I knew deep down that no one could ever make me whole again. I wished I could die in my tears.

The next day, I went to work. I was really pushing myself because I wasn't well. I had a meeting that morning, and by midday, I started having agonizing cramps. I urgently left the office. I called my gynecologist, and I told him I wasn't ok. He told me to come right away. My job site was far away from the road, and I couldn't get a taxi. I didn't care. I started walking as fast as I could. I was sweating. My heart was racing. I was dizzy, and I knew I would have passed out on that street if one of the company's drivers hadn't picked me up and dropped me at the clinic. On our way to the clinic, when he asked me what was wrong, I just told him I was sick. I would rather die than tell anyone what was truly happening to me. So, here I am in that office again, lying on that bed. My gynecologist went through the procedure a second time to make sure this time I was cleaned and cleared. I took the afternoon off again and came back the following week.

Every day, I'd cry myself to sleep. To make the situation worse for me, one month after my abortion, I got let go from my job. I had a verbal promise that by the end of my internship, I'd have a secure job contract, and it didn't happen. That afternoon in the HR office was tough. I got home that day, not knowing what to do with myself. When Michael came back from work, he didn't know what to say. He tried consoling me, but I was too broken to be fixed. What was then for me the point of the abortion if my job was no more? In the months that followed, I stayed home, meditating on my existence most of the time. I didn't know if I'd ever be pregnant again in my life. I went into a deep and very dark hole of depression and sorrow. I couldn't blame anybody but myself for my choices. No day would go by without me crying and hoping that I would have an accident and die because, for me, I deserved it. Sometimes, however, when I had the courage to, I'd whisper a shy "Please, God, forgive me." Till today, sometimes I'll think about that child I never had, and my heart will break once more.

If there's one thing this episode of my life has taught me, it is to own my choices and stand for them. Culture today tends to glorify abortion, and that, to me, is crazy. According to the Google Dictionary, 'Abortion is a deliberate termination of a human pregnancy, most often performed during the first 28 weeks of pregnancy'. Whether you knew or not that there was life inside of you, it doesn't change the fact that a human life, an innocent one for that matter, was terminated. Sounds a lot to me like murder. The notion of 1st, 2nd, and 3rd-degree murder here can make sense. It is my body, therefore, and I can do whatever I want. I was raped; therefore, I'm not going to keep it. I am so scared of what people would say or think. There are so many reasons out there why a woman or a man would want an abortion to happen, but because I have been through it, I can say it is a traumatic experience. It has the power to guilt you for years to come and throw you into a deep hole of shame and depression. In the worst-case scenario, you might never get pregnant again in your life.

Then, one day, Michael thought it would be good for me to start golf. He believed it would help me have some things to look forward to. I loved golfing. It was very therapeutic to my soul, and unlike my preconception of golf, it was more strategic and tough than I had thought it was. Michael would spoil me and get me all types of golf gear I needed and did not need. We both played at almost all the golf fields in Cameroon. I started to enjoy life again, even though there was a hole and a fear in me I felt could only be filled with another pregnancy.

It is only Jesus' love that was able to redeem and restore me. Today, I know that my aborted baby is in Heaven, and that gives me peace because one day, I'll get to see her, too when my time comes to go back home to our Father. His love for me rescued me. When I didn't deserve to be loved, He loved me. He called me by His name, and He didn't define me by my sin. So, who is man to judge and condemn me? *Who shall bring any charge against God's elect? It is God who justifies. Who is to condemn? Christ Jesus is the one who died—more than that, who was raised— who is at the right hand of God, who indeed is interceding for us.* Romans 8:33-34 [ESV]

God shone the light on my sin and said, "Come, I will make you whole again. No matter what, I still love you."

NOT MINE BUT YOURS

Lord, I am not mine, but yours alone.

Let your will be done and not my own.

Put me where you will and let me serve.

In everything I do, let me endure.

This is my prayer, Lord, to you,

My promise and my vow, strong and true.

And the covenant I make on earth,

Let it be fulfilled in heaven. Amen.

John Wesley – Covenant Prayer

It all started on a Saturday morning. We felt freaky, so we decided to have some fun. I watched my period and ovulation very closely, thanks to the app Flo I used at the time – and still do. I didn't know if it would end up in a pregnancy. I hoped hard it would, but I tried not to give it much thought to avoid being disappointed.

Meanwhile, we kept playing golf, and for the first time that year, Michael decided not to go back to the US for his vacation. He said he'd stay with me and started looking into spending vacation in Sao

Tome and Principe. After a week or two of research, he had me book our flights while he secured a resort bungalow on a paradise island in Sao Tome for us. We stayed there for about a week, and oh goodness, it was nice! Every single night, we'd go to bed drunk and wake up at the pool bar. We did some hiking as well and stood on the Equator line. It was so cool. The only thing I regretted not doing was snorkeling. Michael was too drunk that morning to do it with me, and he wouldn't let me go with the Spanish instructor because he was jealous. That was a miserable day for me. But overall, that trip was fun and memorable.

The night we came back from vacation, I felt sick. My stomach was hurting, and I thought it was all that alcohol we took coming back at me. I didn't know yet, but I was pregnant. After a couple of days of still not feeling good, I decided perhaps I should take a pregnancy test. It came out positive. I was going to have a baby. This time, I knew better to listen to myself. It was my second chance to rewrite the story of my pregnancy, and I was determined to do it on my own terms. Michael was very happy when I told him about the pregnancy, but nothing beats the reaction of our best friend, Ornella. Oh, my goodness!!! It was priceless. She was the first person we announced the pregnancy to, and her joyful scream was everything. By that time, our friendship had grown and strengthened over the months after my abortion. I never told her about that. It was a secret only my mom, Michael's mom, and Corine knew.

You watched me as I was being formed in utter seclusion, as I was woven together in the dark of the womb. You saw me before I was born. Every day of my life was recorded in your book. Every moment was laid out before a single day had passed. Psalm 139:15-16 [NLT]

When I was initially thinking about how I'll write this chapter, Hannah in the Bible came to my spirit. If you've never read or heard about her story, she's the lady who consecrated her son, Samuel, way before he was even conceived or born. She's been childless for a very long time and promised God that if He gives her a child, she'll give him back to Him.

Before Caleb's conception, I was pregnant. That first pregnancy, from the very moment I gave it up, I was affected by a feeling of profound sorrow. No week will pass by without me asking God to forgive me. In fact, I didn't even believe that I was forgiven. I thought I'd never be pregnant again. I heard stories of women who aborted once and never again got pregnant. I thought this was going to be my story as well. However, in my tears and sorrow, I would beg God not only to forgive me but to please give me a second chance. In those prayers, I promised Him that my son would be His and not mine. Like Hannah, I constantly consecrated my yet unconceived and unborn child.

When I got pregnant for the second time, though it was still out of wedlock and away from my Christian values, first, I knew that was an answered prayer, but second, I knew this child was God's, not mine. I had to learn how to detach emotionally and mentally, in a healthy way, of course, from my son way before I saw him in person. I get attached to people easily; I love to be there and spend time with the people I love. Understand that my love languages are Quality Time and Physical Touch. I needed to train myself on how to love my son the right way. I needed to understand that he's not mine but God's. I needed to let go of the control that parents tend to have on their kids.

I'm grateful today that my husband and I raised Caleb to be independent. We had all the reasons to be overly protective of him, but I made a promise to God, and I cared about following it through. I prayed for this child to come into our lives, yet I knew he wasn't our 'property'.

Monday, June 27, 2016, a little before 2 p.m., I gave birth to my son Caleb. That was the best day of my life. Even my wedding after that didn't beat the joy I had on this day. Caleb was considered a big baby, very healthy, and a very beautiful one. I think most newborns are ugly, except for my brother, Cedric – the cutest baby I had seen by then in pictures. So, no, Caleb didn't escape my critical eye. It was in his second month that I started seeing his beauty, and by the time he turned five months, I was drop-dead in love with how handsome that little boy was.

One night, Caleb was sleeping in his crib, and I was just staring at him. The things we do as parents are interesting. We're delighted by the simple things our kids do, especially in their early years. Watching him breathe filled me with a joy I can't explain. To me, he was like a masterpiece. I loved him with all my heart. Sometimes, I wondered how something so perfect could come from someone as imperfect as me. He was my mini-version, with a skin tone closer to that of the colonizers. My blood flowed through his veins. To me, nothing compared to the feeling of procreating. Occasionally, my mom would look at me, then hug me and say, "I gave birth to you," as if she were saying, "I love you so much, and I'm in awe of what came from me; I'm so proud."

As I felt the butterflies in my belly for my son that night, I heard a voice in my spirit: "No matter what you do, even if you commit the biggest crime, I would never stop loving you, and you would always be my child." It struck me like a revelation. I realized this was God speaking to me. I fell to the ground and started crying, inconsolable. I replayed the film of my life from the past six years in my mind. For the first time in many years, I confessed my sins to Him wholeheartedly, and for the second and last time, I made Jesus the King over my life, never to take it back again.

The rest of my week, through my interactions with my son, taught me a lot about God's love for me. After everything I did, He never stopped loving and seeing me as His daughter and so desperately, like the prodigal, wanted me back home. I imagined how broken His heart might have been when He used to hear me whisper these words to myself, walking under the hot midday sun in Douala (Houston's summer heat is the worst I've experienced so far, though). "Get some practice, Corine, and be used to this heat because hell, where you are going to, will be worse." At that time, my knowledge of God had become so weak that the enemy had gained ground in my mind, convincing me that I was too dirty to be forgiven and that my place was with him in hell, which I finally accepted, though it terrified me to the core of my being. The picture I had of God back in those days was an always angry father, ready to condemn you whenever you make a mistake. That's how pastors in Cameroon made us see God. I didn't know much about how deep His love for me was. The culture in which I grew up depicted a father that way – one you need to constantly fear. One you can't question or have open conversations with. One you can't approach freely. One who never spoke softly but was always angry. So, I guess it just felt normal for pastors to preach about a whooping God. Unfortunately, it still happens that way back home in some churches, thankfully not all.

My son, though conceived and born out of wedlock, was my opening door back into the house of the Lord. Since then, I have had episodes where I've been disobedient to God. The difference today and since 2016 is I know that because of Jesus' sacrifice on the cross, my identity as a believer is no longer attached to the sins I commit. *Day after day every priest stands and performs his religious duties; again and again he offers the same sacrifices, which can never take away sins. But when this priest had offered for all time one sacrifice for sins, he sat down at the right hand of God, ... For by one sacrifice he has made perfect forever those who are being made holy.* Hebrews 10:11-12,14 [NIV]. It is because of God's redemption and restoration power that we can stand in the assurance of His unfailing love for us, no matter what. *Can anything ever separate us from Christ's love? Does it mean he no longer loves us if we have trouble or calamity, or are persecuted, or hungry, or destitute, or in danger, or threatened with death?* Romans 8:35

[NLT]

When Caleb started getting into things around the house, we used to just let him do his stuff and learn his lessons. We'll let him fall and watch how he'll stand up and continue. As a child, he'll get himself into all kinds of stuff, and we'll let him be a child. There were things and situations we'd protect him from getting into, of course, but ultimately, we were raising a strong and independent boy, and he was our pride and our joy.

In every stage of Caleb's existence and progression, God taught me life lessons. That's when I came to realize that even God doesn't always come to the rescue whenever we have a little fall. As you grow up, challenges in life look different, and they're for sure tougher. If you're constantly sheltered, how will you be able to stand for yourself? And this is where I admire my husband. He's so strong. From the stories he shared with me about his life when he was younger, he was a wild, daredevil boy. Not only did all his experiences build a physically strong man, but he's also so open-minded that he'll figure out a way of making things work for him, no matter the environment he finds himself in. That's the kind of man I knew Caleb would be.

Every single time, I'll tell Caleb that mommy and daddy will never love him as much as God does. I'll tell him to never love me or my husband more than he loves God. Sometimes, I'll tell him what career I'd love for him to do, but I'll always end by saying that I'll respect what God calls him to be and hope that we'll not get into conflict about it. I knew I had to learn how to respect and accept God's decisions in the life of my son. As a parent who loves their children, it is so difficult to release your authority on your children over God's authority. I'm grateful for how easy it was for me, though, to make God's authority in Caleb's life come before mine. I intend to raise my future children this way as well. God should always come before us, their parents.

The strength with which I trusted God with Caleb's life was unbelievable, even to myself. I worried about nothing when it came to Caleb. And when I say nothing, I mean it! You could see it in my actions. Some friends of mine voiced out to me one time how amazed they were at my attitude and the carefree upbringing of my son. Even on the day Caleb left to be with Jesus, I remember sending a message to Ornella when we got to the urgent care that morning that we were here, asking her not to worry and that we'd be home by the end of the day. She was another mommy to Caleb, and in almost three years of existence, Caleb had never been sick. So, I needed to reassure her. Little did I know at the time that he wouldn't go back home with us. I knew that no matter what came Caleb's way, God would be there for him. *For this is what the Lord Almighty says: "After the Glorious One has sent me against the nations that have plundered you—for whoever touches you touches the apple of his eye* Zechariah 2:8 [NIV]. I mean, take a minute and think about it. You are the apple of His eye; don't you think that in all ways, He'll fiercely show up for you?

To trust God is to surrender fully to Him. To be able to surrender is to know who God is. Knowing God is about having that intimate relationship through prayers and devoted Bible reading time. Caleb was never ours. He was God's very own ambassador, and he accomplished what God appointed him to do in this world.

Listen to Me, you island, and pay attention, you people from afar. The Lord called Me from the womb; From the body of My mother, He named Me. Isaiah 49:1 [NASB]

Caleb's life was in his heavenly father's hands, and no one had a better say on him than Him, Abba Father. That's why I was able, as a mom, to see my son, not as mine but as God's child, one He entrusted Michael and me to raise.

READY FOR THE NEXT CHALLENGE

I wanna be tried by fire

Purifier

You take whatever you desire

Lord here's my life

Clean my hands, purify my heart

I wanna burn for you, only for You

Take my life as a sacrifice

I wanna burn for you, only for You

Refiner – Maverick City

When Abba Father rescued me back to Him in 2016, He had been teaching me His love. When I moved to the US in 2018, I had plenty of time to dive into the world, strengthen my spiritual being, and get to know Him more and that part of who He is. There is this song from 'Hillsong – It's Your Love'; every time I think about how God rescued me, I always say that if not for His love, I wouldn't be standing and talking about Him.

The year Caleb passed away, though I was going through deep sorrow, one thing remained: I knew for a fact that God was love, and His love for me was real. Sometimes, when I was crying, I'd say, "If you really loved me, then why did you let it happen?" However, deep down, I knew so strongly that He loved me. God is so intentional about the things He does in our lives. Today, I know and believe that for Him to take Caleb, He had to make sure that my understanding of His love for me was grounded. So, the Holy Spirit taught me the depth of His love for me, but also how to extend love to others. I believe it is from that time that I learned how to extend grace to others.

When I moved to the US, I was so hungry to know God. I wasn't working, wasn't going to school, had no friends to talk to except my loved ones back home, and having to adjust to their time zone was hard. When they were up, it was sleeping time in the US. When they slept, it was daytime in the US. I was living my life for the most part in their time zone, but then it became difficult because I had a one-and-a-half-year-old boy to take care of. I couldn't sleep in the day and be awake in the night just because I wanted company from my loved ones back home. It was very frustrating to me. It felt like my friends back home were moving forward with their lives and I was still holding back on my life back home. I didn't have a cell phone number during the first two months, so I was limited in what I could do and go. Walking around the neighborhood with my son in his stroller was the only way I could move from one point to another. I can't even start telling you how miserable it feels sometimes to walk under that hot Houston sun. All these greatly contributed to my unhappiness during the first months in Houston. Every evening, when Michael came back home, I'd cry and threaten him that I would go back home to Cameroon because I was too sad and too lonely in this country. Until one night, he got so fed up with me – apparently, I wasn't even trying to feel better – that he told me he'd buy my plane ticket back to Cameroon. Though he didn't say he'd stop me from taking Caleb with me, I knew there was no way he'd let me leave with Caleb. That day, I decided to stop my complaints and do my best to appreciate being here in the US.

From there, I changed my habits. I stopped staying up all night on WhatsApp with my loved ones in Cameroon. I created a schedule that would work for me, and all the empty hours I had after doing my chores and taking care of Caleb, I'd spend them reading my bible, praying, or reading self-help books. It is funny how true the statement 'When God wants to take you to another level of knowing Him, He'll isolate you, so He has your full attention'. My friendship with the Holy Spirit exponentially grew from here. It was also around that time that Martha became my spiritual partner and one of my closest friends till today. Even though she was in Cameroon, we were able to find a suitable time for both of us to pray and exchange. I met her years ago from our youth church back home. I was older than her, and I never suspected that one day she'd be my friend. My sister, for that matter. Nonetheless, I had always admired how simple she was. She once told me, as our friendship grew, that she didn't like me when we were younger and that I seemed to be snobbish. That was behind us now, because it was the beginning of what God wanted for our relationship.

One of the things the Holy Spirit was adamant about teaching me was the importance of challenges and understanding that it will always be part of my walk with the Lord. Challenges come not to destroy us but to strengthen our spirit and to make us mature in Christ. So, He took me back to the first challenge I experienced as a believer – a false accusation from my very own spiritual father – and encouraged me to forgive him truly. He was the reason why, for years, I've run away from the church. But now that I was connecting with the Holy Spirit, I was able to see how I could have addressed the situation differently and not remained in the offended mindset. When the time for me to join a new church where I could commune with other believers and once again serve came, it was hard. I wanted to let go of that pain, but I was scared I'd be hurt and offended again. Nonetheless, I ended up surrendering my pain to the Lord, letting Him fill me with His peace, and my quest to join a church started.

By then, Michael, Caleb, and I moved to a new apartment in the Northwest side of Houston. I remembered searching for Pentecostal churches near me because that's what I was used to. Strangely, the pictures that popped up on Google didn't reassure me, so I wouldn't dare visit those churches. One time in my research, I saw 'non-denominational churches', and I wondered what that was. I had never heard that expression before. So, I decided to make a list of five non-denominational churches around me. I planned to visit them all and decide which one would be my home church. The first Sunday, I planned to visit the first one on my list. For some reason, I ignored it; I never did. Throughout that week, there was this church, New Life Church on Hammerly Boulevard, whose building was intriguing to me. It was a dome shape. I had never seen that before. Here I am in the Uber by myself, on my way to that church the following Sunday. I sat in the church and kept looking around. I was scared. The service had not started yet, but they were playing Christian songs I used to listen to when I was a teenager, newly baptized in Christ. Non-denominational church, what do they mean by that? I questioned. Will they sacrifice me at some point? Are they serious with God? As I was asking myself all types of questions, I heard the Holy Spirit say, "Who are you to judge my people?" I didn't need any more words. These were God's people. The service was great that Sunday, and I felt good there. And just like that, New Life Church became my home church in Houston.

For God is pleased when, conscious of his will, you patiently endure unjust treatment. 1 Peter 2:19 [NLT]. When someone is unfair to you, whether the person is in the church or not, your attitude towards them or the situation is to look up to God to be your Jehovah Tsidkenu – The Lord of your righteousness. Back in the day, I used to believe that because someone is in the church, then they should always act right. Though this is what is required from us believers, to be examples, it doesn't always happen that way. The church is like a hospital. We're there because we're sick! We need God because we acknowledge we can't do without Him. Someone might have been struggling with lying. The person comes to church, still does the same things, and hurts someone else. Does that suck? Yes, it does. But the more you mature as a believer, the more your level of compassion and forgiveness grows till you get to a point where you're capable of forgiving someone even before they ask for forgiveness and stop the cycle of hatred at your level.

Other human beings should not cause us to leave the church or abandon God. We are part of God's church, belonging to Him alone. Once I realized this, no one ever had the power to drive me away from a church. If I ever leave, it won't be out of anger towards someone, but because I feel God calling me elsewhere. This understanding presents a tough challenge that many Christians struggle with. It's far too easy to blame others for our problems, leading to what my aunt described as 'church hopping' - constantly moving from one church to another. However, we must remember that it's our responsibility to handle situations maturely. Avoid the trap of self-pity and constant complaining for sympathy. Choose instead to brush off any offenses, show compassion to those who hurt you, and maintain your focus on Christ.

Every challenge we encounter is not meant to destroy us but to strengthen and grow our faith. *Consider it pure joy, my brothers and sisters, whenever you face trials of many kinds, because you know that the testing of your faith produces perseverance.* James 1:2-3 [NIV] We, as Christians, should expect and even welcome these challenges. How else will we grow and become more Christ-like if not refined by adversity? Just as students undergo final exams to advance to the next level, so do believers face trials to deepen their relationship with the Lord and gain new revelations of who He is.

The more I studied God's word, the more I grew in my faith. In my baby faith stage − when I first gave my life to Christ − I used to think that as a believer, life was going to be smooth and perfect. I'll be on a soft white cloud all day, every day, and nothing negative will come my way. But just like a baby graduate from breastmilk and formula to solid food, so should our progress be as believers. However, I was not prepared for some of the realities of what following Christ looked like − dying to myself and enduring hardship. Truth be told, it can be very depressing at times to live a life that pleases God. You lose friends who don't understand your choices. You're being called judgmental when all you do is speak the truth; even when you do it in love, you're not welcome anymore. Jesus himself was being called a man of great sorrow. Why would you think that as His own, you won't partake in His suffering?

The reason why someone was able to shake my faith to the point of leaving the church in Cameroon was because I wasn't prepared and taught about challenges. It took me about six years in the world to get back into the house of the Lord one day. The Holy Spirit, therefore, needed to make sure that I understood and accepted that challenges will always be part of my walk with Him because they will grow me as a believer in what He has called me to become. In those moments, He will always be by my side because His unconditional love for me will carry me through and will make the burden lighter. Once I understood that, I started seeing my life as a believer in a very different way. I started desiring to know Him more, to go into a higher dimension of my relationship with him. To serve Him in everything I do, to lay my life down as a living sacrifice, holy and acceptable to Him [Romans 12:1].

As the Holy Spirit was teaching me about challenges, I was going through one, which was believing that Michael and I would get married, just as He promised me when we left Cameroon. God knew I didn't want to find myself in an adulterous situation anymore. I wanted my life and actions to be an example to those looking up to me [Matthew 5:16 NIV]. I wanted to be married. I wanted to do things right. The problem was that Michael had sworn to me that he'd never get married again. 'Over his dead body', he insinuated. He had been married for ten years before, and things ended up in a very sour way. It left him broken emotionally, morally, and financially. Trusting a woman or fully investing in her wasn't something he was willing to do again. The repercussion on me and our relationship wasn't something I deserved. I didn't break his heart or mistreat him. I wasn't with him for his money or his status. Yet, I was here, paying the price for someone else's selfishness. When hurt people hurt people, the hurting cycle becomes difficult to handle. That is why it is important to heal from a breakup before engaging in any other type of relationship, or those hurting feelings will come and haunt you and the new person you're in a relationship with.

The company Michael used to work for in Cameroon was shutting down its offices, so he had to be relocated back to the US. That's why he wanted Caleb and I to go with him as a family. I absolutely did not want to go. My initial response was to tell him that there was no way I was going to move my life to someone who was just my boyfriend, even if he was the father of my son. Moreover, at that point, I didn't care about our relationship because we had been going through a tough time. I didn't feel the relationship anymore, and it had been that way for quite some time now. I couldn't take it to be with someone who didn't value me or wanted to build something with me. It was easier to handle it while being in Cameroon because I had my loved ones and activities I could escape to. But what was that going to be like in a country that was foreign to me and where I knew almost no one?

Nonetheless, I decided to pray about it. Should I go or should I stay? Should I stay in a relationship, I believed wouldn't end up in marriage? Not only was my heart broken because I couldn't understand why Michael would 'hate' me that much to the point of not wanting to marry me but to be so cold to me the way he used to.

At the same time, I felt like, as a believer, I couldn't allow myself to continue this relationship. I thought, what if I want to share God's love or word with someone, and they come back at me like, "You're living with a man who isn't your husband, yet you tell us what to do with our spiritual life? Go fix yours first".

I had been praying for some time now, yet I didn't get an answer on whether I was to move with him or not. One afternoon, I couldn't handle it anymore. I was determined to have an answer from the Lord. I told my nanny not to disturb me, no matter what happened to Caleb. After a couple of hours of prayers, I heard in my spirit Joshua 1:9. 'Wherever I'd go, He'd be with me'. Deep down in my spirit, I had hoped that He would tell me to stay in Cameroon, but He didn't. How could God ask me to move with a man who wasn't my husband? For days, I wondered. Until one day, He spoke to my heart again. I wrote down in my journal what He said. Here it is *"Yes, I am a God of principles. I have standards, and I abide by them. But I'm also letting you go because I am not a God of disorder. Because you've had a child with him already, I do not wish for you to move to another man. He will be the father of all your children. I will turn your sin, your mistake, into a testimony. I will change His heart about marriage, and you will become his wife. Trust me and see me work things out. Go, I am with you."*

At that point in my life, to be honest, I wasn't in love with Michael anymore. I was so unhappy being with him. So I cried bitterly. I was crushed. I was sad. Why would God let me go with a man I didn't care for anymore? Mind you, this was the second time the Lord confirmed to me His desire for me to move to the US with Michael and Caleb. So, we finally moved to the US. Despite it all, I didn't stop praying and believing that God would do what He said He'd do. I was looking up to Him to see how he would change this situation. Six months into moving to the US, Michael and I got married. This miracle made me realize how God is capable of changing people's hearts. Michael didn't become a better person right away. Our relationship didn't become the best, but that was the beginning of what God has started doing in both our lives and marriage. The best is still yet to come, and I believe He will complete what He has started already in my husband's life.

Way before I got married, I started sharing my walk with Christ on social media. I was authentic about the struggles I faced and how my sole focus was Jesus. Sometimes, it was a struggle for me to believe that God approved of me despite living unmarried with a man. To believe that God could change someone's heart was a struggle. Yet it happened. In these moments, I came to understand that God was pleased by my sincere desire to honor Him in my life. God acts in people's lives differently. God can change a sinful situation like mine for His glory. In other cases, He might request a dissolution of the relationship. The most important thing to do is to always seek His perfect plan for your life, even if it doesn't make sense now. I have been asked a couple of times what my position on cohabitating with a partner before marriage is, and my answer has been and will always be – "what does the Bible say about it?" It is something I don't encourage. If we call ourselves believers, there are standards we're required to live up to. However, if we fall into a sinful trap, God, in his unending love, will gracefully redeem us and use the situation for a positive outcome. But again, as a believer, you should desire holiness and seek God's perfect will for your life.

Two days after my wedding, it was my birthday. On that day, I was on the phone with my cousin Viviane, talking about God's ways of doing things, the challenges we face as believers, and how it grows us in our faith. Towards the end of our call, I told God in her presence, "Lord, I'm ready for the next challenge, but please not death." We both laughed. Then she said, "My dear, please enjoy this wedding testimony first. It is well deserved. Don't worry about challenges for now." By that time, I had embraced challenges in my walk with Christ. I knew that no matter what came my way, with God by my side, I could overcome it and discover a new face of who He is. The only challenge I feared could overthrow me was death. And that's exactly what He decided to throw my way.

JESUS WHERE WERE YOU?

In the waiting, in the searching

In the healing and the hurting

Like a blessing buried in the broken pieces

Every minute, every moment

Of where I've been and where I'm going

Even when I didn't know it

Or couldn't see it

There was Jesus

There Was Jesus – Zach Williams & Dolly Parton

Nothing prepared me for what I was going to encounter that morning.

Jesus, to me, had always been the serious, almost cold guy I knew from the movie "Jesus" recorded in 1979, where Brian Deacon represented Jesus. All my life, that is who I envisioned Jesus to be, so much so that not even the Jesus in "The Passion of Christ", played by Jim Caviezel, could make me divert from that first Jesus. It was in 2016 when I gave my life to Christ for the 'second and last' time – believers will understand me here – that I came to know a completely different Jesus. Though I still believed Him to be a very serious guy, it was His sweet, soft, and unconditional love that changed my perception and knowledge of Him upside down. This Jesus, in His demeanor, looked more like the Jesus from the show "The Chosen" – I hadn't watched The Chosen by then yet.

I was in my bed, sobbing, thinking about Caleb, and wondering why this had to happen to me. What did I do to deserve this? I had read time and again that Jesus would never leave us, but I felt lonely and abandoned. I can't even explain how broken my heart felt that morning. All I can remember is, at some point, I screamed to the top of my lungs, "JESUS, WHERE WERE YOU WHEN CALEB DIED?". Then I lowered my voice and continued, "Didn't you say in your word that you will never abandon us? Why did you abandon me that afternoon? Why were you not there?" As much as I believed the Bible to be true, I couldn't help but wonder if perhaps the Gospel was a lie. Over the course of my relationship with the Lord, and by observing other people around me, I've come to realize how interesting we are sometimes to question the validity of the Bible when we go through a difficult time in our lives.

As I'm writing and reading my cry to the Lord out loud that morning, it all sounds so familiar. Remember when Mary and Martha cried to Jesus about Lazarus's death? There's truly nothing new under the sun. I had never asked myself the question until today if Jesus also cried when hearing me cry out as he cried when he was before Lazarus' sisters [John 11:35]. I will never know, and it doesn't matter because what happened next completely reshaped my vision and knowledge of who Jesus is to me.

As I was sitting in my bed, tears whipped, and my eyes closed; I felt a presence at the edge of my bed as if someone was standing. I couldn't open my eyes because I knew in my spirit that something I could have never imagined in my wildest dreams was happening. Jesus was in my bedroom.

"Where do you want me to sit? Or do you prefer that I stand here?" He politely asked me.

"Come sit next to me in the bed." And again, I felt his presence on my bed. The entire time, my eyes stayed closed. It was like I was in a dream, but I was awake. The conversation wasn't audible. It was our spirits speaking to each other.

"You asked where I was, and I've come to show you what happened that day. This time, I'll show you the spiritual reality of that day. Do you want to see it?"

"Yes, please! Show me!"

"Ok, let's do it."

Caleb hugged me tightly, not wanting to let go. By that time, we had already spent the entire day there, and the nurse was about to remove his IV and discharge us just before this hug. Then, the doctor arrived, insisting on keeping us hospitalized for reasons that I found unsettling. I texted my husband, trying to convey what the doctor had said. Physically, this was the situation. Spiritually, however, Caleb's hug marked the beginning of his journey from earth to heaven. It was his goodbye to me.

Today, I am grateful for that warm hug from my son before

he departed. I am also relieved that my husband, Michael, wasn't present in the room to witness this. It would have been agonizing for him, as this would have been the second time he had lost a loved one named Caleb in his arms; the first being his younger brother. I cannot fathom the pain of losing a brother, as all of mine are alive. But the horrific feeling of holding your only child in your arms as he takes his last breath is a pain I know all too well. My son entered this world in my arms and left it in the same loving embrace, nearly three years apart. I would never have wished for Michael to endure the trauma of losing his son in such a manner.

This chapter of my book is probably the most difficult to write because it takes me back to the day Caleb left us. And even though I know he's with Jesus in a peaceful place and that one day we'll get to see him again, I'm still hurt deep inside because I miss him, and I don't know when I'll get to see him. On Monday, June 27, 2022, I wrote the first draft of this chapter, and on that day, I realized waking up that morning that I gave birth to Caleb Monday, June 27, 2016. It is Monday for me. It might not mean anything to anybody, but it does to me. My son would have been six years old on the dot, and coincidentally, that's the day I finally decided to write this book! Three years after his death.

When Caleb passed away, my husband wrote down, in April of 2019, the story of what happened. I had initially recorded an audio of the series of events that took place that Monday, March 11, 2019, but I couldn't find it. However, the entry below is the most accurate description we kept of how Caleb left that day.

I asked my wife what had happened leading up to him not breathing. She told me that the nurse had come in and started to remove Caleb's splint so she could remove his IV and said he would be going home soon. However, the doctor came into the room and told her he wanted to extend the stay by 6 to 8 more hours. She said the nurse was in the room, too, and she (my wife) had the feeling that the nurse wasn't really in agreement with the doctor, but she guessed that since he was her superior, she couldn't display her objection in front of her (my wife). That's when she sent me a text to inform me about extending Caleb's stay. She told me our son wanted her to lay her head on top of his, like using her as a shade from the light (because he was sleeping, and the light was disturbing him) and him holding her by the neck, and they were alone in the room. She said as she was "shading" him, she heard the sound of air inside him. She told me it was such a strange noise that she looked up and realized that the IV was empty and rushed to the door to call for someone to come and remove it. The doctor was the first person to come in. She told me as she was holding our son in her arms and asking the doctor to remove it, he had a "stroke", and our son started turning green and brown. She told me she begged the doctor to remove it, but he didn't want to remove the IV, though he was witnessing what was happening. She told me he kept telling her, "Ma'am, I can't remove it because we may need it to help him since he's having a reaction." She said his chest suddenly lunged up in the bed and that he seemed to start breathing only one more time, then stopped again shortly after (3 times this breathing "fight" happened). The doctor called in the nurse, and they attempted to reanimate him. This is when my wife left the room to text me that our baby was undergoing CPR.

Soon after I sent my husband the text, the 911 emergency team came in and were performing CPR. Michael, too, came in from his doctor's appointment, and we were together in the hallway, close to our son's bedroom. I was kneeling on the floor, all shaken and praying. I didn't know what to pray or how to pray. All I did was pray in the spirit (as Christians say, "in tongues") as hard as I could while there was action taking place in my son's bedroom.

So, this is what Jesus showed me was happening in the spiritual realm.

In my son's room, Jesus was there, standing calm when Caleb held onto me. The atmosphere was very peaceful. When Caleb gasped three times, Jesus was standing at the top left corner of the bed. When I was asked to leave the room so that they could perform the rescue, Jesus stayed in the room with them. This time, He wasn't as calm. He looked like a football coach giving instructions to his players on the field. Indeed, He wasn't alone in the room. I saw two angels to whom He asked not to leave Caleb's side. Then He took the Holy Spirit on the side and told Him to fully empower me as I was on my knees in the hallway praying and wondering what I was going to tell my family back home. At that point, I saw the Holy Spirit bending forward behind me with his hands on my shoulder and screaming in a deep and loud voice, "Power! Power! Power!". Three times, He said it. Suddenly, it was like the heavens opened, and too many angels for me to count were cheering and encouraging me and declaring that this event would not overtake me, but I'd make it through this season with the power from above.

When the paramedics decided to take Caleb into the ambulance to the hospital, they asked me if I wanted to go with him. I said no. I was too scared, too in shock, to be able to stand next to him and possibly see him suffer if at all he did. For a long time after Caleb left, I felt guilty and blamed myself for not getting into the ambulance. I thought, perhaps if I went with him in the ambulance, I'd have prayed some more and saved his life. The truth, though, was that God had a different plan I had yet to uncover and understand. In the vision, I saw the two huge angles getting into the ambulance car with him.

"That's when they took Caleb's soul away," Jesus whispered to me as the vision was coming to an end. Every reanimation that happened after that at the hospital, Caleb wasn't there anymore. He was gone to be with Jesus.

I couldn't believe everything that I saw. I couldn't believe that Jesus would step down in my bedroom and show me what happened that way. Like Mercy Chinwo, the Nigerian Gospel singer says in her song Excess Love, "Who am I that you're mindful of me?" Who was I, really, that He'd take the time to reveal this to me? Who was I?

"Jesus, did I just make this all up? Did you really show me this?" I was a little confused as to whether this was from God or from my imagination, which, at this point, we can agree was wild.

"What do you think?" He gently asked while smiling.

"I don't know! I'm not sure! I think what you showed me was real, but no one will ever believe me when I say you were here, and you showed me this. They'll say I'm crazy." I wasn't ready for what He'll say next.

"Aren't you crazy then?" He burst out laughing.

I laughed out loud, too, because this was something to laugh about.

"You, my people, are crazy to the world. To me, you are not crazy. They don't understand what you experience with me, so they call it craziness."

I nodded my head in agreement.

A person who does not have the Spirit does not accept the truths that come from the Spirit of God. That person thinks they are foolish and cannot understand them, because they can only be judged to be true by the Spirit. 1 Corinthians 2:14 [NCV]

"What you saw today, you know deep inside of you that it is real. You know I was here in your bedroom today, and now you know I was also there when Caleb left. I will always be there wherever you go. Never forget that. I never left, and I will never leave you."

"Jesus, you're so different from what I thought you were. You are so funny, so simple, and actually very handsome and sexy." I giggled. "Thanks so much for your visit today."

In Matthew 28:20, Jesus said He'll be with us till the end of ages. It was a promise, and He is faithful to his word. Today, I have a firm assurance that He walks this life with me every single day, even when I sometimes forget to acknowledge it. Meeting Jesus that morning in my bedroom was the best thing to date I had ever experienced in my walk with the Lord. Indeed, He is close to the brokenhearted.

While we were at the urgent care, I sent a message to my church leaders asking them to pray for Caleb as they were performing CPR on him. I texted my mom, too, back in Cameroon, asking her to pray. Because of the time difference, she didn't answer my texts or my calls. The paramedics tried to stabilize his situation, and from there, we all rushed to the hospital. Pastor Mary and Pastor Brett from New Life Church had been waiting for us there, unfortunately, on the wrong side of the hospital, so we couldn't see them. There had been times after that I wished I was able to send them my exact location, and they would have come and prayed over Caleb's body so that he would resurrect. I regretted it bitterly, but then I consoled myself by thinking that, with all the adrenaline rush in my body, I couldn't think straight to share my exact location with them. Perhaps that wasn't God's plan either.

When we arrived at the hospital, Caleb was rushed into the emergency room while Michael and I were in the waiting room. I had never seen in my life as many nurses and doctors on one patient. I used to see it in movies, and never in my darkest nightmares would I imagine going through this. For a very long time after that, any time I'd hear a paramedic siren, it would trigger me, and no matter where I'd hear it from, I'd stop and cry myself a river. A couple of friends from church, Chris and Loretta, and Mike's relatives, Uncle Tony and Aunt Dollie, were with us in the waiting room. Minutes felt like hours, and it was like my body was decomposing. I sat there crying in my heart, "God, please don't let my son die. I know you can save him. Please, I'm begging you, don't let anything happen to him. I want us to go back home together". Then the doctor in charge came to the waiting room and told Michael and me that they did everything they could, but Caleb wasn't going to come back and invited us to come and say our last goodbye. Michael hit the wall and injured his fingers. As we were walking towards the emergency room where Caleb was lying, I was crying and whispering in my heart, "Lord, please resurrect Caleb." We went in, and I saw my son, my baby, lying there lifeless. I was so weak. I wished the earth would open and swallow me. I wanted to die so badly. How was I ever going to live without Caleb? What will my life be without him? We both took turns and said our goodbyes. We stayed at the hospital for a couple more minutes to fill up some paperwork that would allow them to carry out a forensic autopsy – it's a procedure done when a toddler dies unexpectedly and unexplained, then left to go back home.

From the hospital to the car in the parking lot, I was walking barefoot like a mad woman. The village it took to raise Caleb till then in Cameroon, I felt like I failed them. What was I going to tell them? Why did I not protect him better? I felt like an incompetent parent. In the couple of weeks that followed, I had some dreams where I was trying to save him and I couldn't, and some dreams where I was able to save him. Michael experienced the same type of dreams. So, we went back home with my friends from church and my husband's uncle and aunt. When I got home, I went straight to Caleb's room. I was inconsolable. I started putting his stuff together. I wanted to get rid of it. I didn't want to see it because it was breaking my heart. Loretta came in, calmed me down, and told me not to do anything that night; my adrenaline rush was too high. She told me about her experience when her mom passed away a couple of years from that time and how tough it was for her and her family. With Chris, they prayed for us, always checking to see how we were handling things. I can never be thankful enough for their love and support. Aunt Dollie suggested we go with them to their house, so Michael and I packed our bags and left with his relatives. Nine months before this tragedy, we were in their backyard in Baytown, celebrating our wedding. Now we were back, but this time, not for a happy event.

The next day, my sister-friend, Fabiola, drove from Austin to Baytown to come see us. Caleb was like a cousin to her daughters, and this tragedy affected her a lot as well. Michael's mom and stepfather arrived the same day, too, from Florida. We all came together to support each other, just like it's done back home when someone loses a loved one. By then, I had spoken to my loved ones back home in Cameroon. I had posted on all my social media platforms that Caleb was gone. Many people knew Caleb through my social media platforms without ever meeting him in person, and I even made new friends online because we shared our journeys as toddler moms together. It was such a horrible time of our lives. One day, my friend April came to visit us when we were still at our relatives' house, and she helped me audio-record what happened the day Caleb passed away. Everything was still so clear in my mind, and I didn't want to forget any details in case that might have been helpful in the future. We had a visit from Pastor Mary and Pastor Brett. The warmth, love, and condolences they brought from the church were so heartwarming. I particularly appreciated when Pastor Mary shared with me the story of when she lost her previous husband and how God didn't want her to resurrect him either, yet showed up for her through the grieving season. Even though grief is different from one person to another, it remains the emptiness, the anger, the guilt, and the loneliness that you experience when a loved one you shared your life with is gone. She gave me a motherly hug and told me it was okay to cry and that it would come like a wave, but God would be my healer.

For a week we stayed there. Every morning when I woke up, I wished I hadn't, and going to bed was hard. I'd cry myself to sleep, hoping to die in my sleep. The first few days, in the middle of the night, Michael would be in the living room and scream his lungs out. It broke my heart to hear my husband sob so bitterly. What made it harder and darker for him was the lack of hope of ever seeing his son. I knew Caleb was in heaven and that one day I'd get to see him, but Michael believed he would never see him, not in this life nor in the life to come. He had issues believing there is life after death. That's why I won't stop praying for my husband to one day accept Jesus as his Lord and Savior. Feeding us was difficult, poor Aunt Dollie. We had no appetite at all, and when we did, a bite or two was enough. How could I eat? Did I even deserve to eat? So much guilt had invaded me. One afternoon, Aunt Dollie took my mother-in-law and me to the park to air our minds. It felt good, though seeing kids at some point was hurting.

By the end of the week, we decided we'd go home and face our new reality – life without Caleb. My mother-in-law and her husband drove us back. I remembered how hard it was for me to let my mother-in-law go back to Florida. During that entire week, she had been so emotionally supportive. She, too, lost her younger son, Caleb, more than a decade ago and was truly the only one I felt could understand better my mother's heart. "Please, Mommy Judy, don't go. Don't leave me," I told her, crying as she was telling Michael and me how important it was for us to face this tragedy. She reminded us that she was just a call away, hugged us, and left to go back to Florida with her husband.

The following week was hell. That's when I wished my mom was there to take care of me and wipe my tears. But every time I called her, I was the one to console her. My mom was devastated. Caleb was the first grandchild she got to build a relationship with. She used to call him all types of names – my treasure, my blessing, my joy, and so much more. One day, when Caleb was still alive and we were living in Cameroon, she admitted to me that she loved Caleb more than she loved me. I remembered how hard I laughed that night. It was so cute to see my mom loving on her grandson.

I bless the Lord for my nephew, Jayden, who was a little less than a year old and became my mom's consolation as she was going through this loss. Jayden showed her love, literally wiped her tears, and made her smile. Today, my mom and he are so attached; it's unbelievable to me at times.

For days, I'd go into Caleb's room and cry. It was like a shrine to me. One afternoon, as I was lying in his bed, I heard the Holy Spirit whisper to me, "This is where you'll find healing". Sure enough, that room became my relaxation room. I took the bed out and repositioned the teepee Caleb got from his Mawmaw – Cajun way of saying grandma, and that became my shelter. I'd lay in there and read, drink a glass of wine, meditate, and cry as I thought about Caleb.

The day Caleb passed away and the weeks that followed were very traumatic. I felt very lonely at first navigating it, questioning and wondering if Jesus didn't hold onto His promise of never leaving us by ourselves. When the biggest waves started to calm down, that's when He showed me otherwise in a vision that He was always there. I didn't experience the resurrection of my son like some people did, but that doesn't make God less of the almighty God that He is. I bless Him for the gift of my son's life and honor His presence in our lives.

EVEN IF HE DOESN'T

There's a grace when the heart is under fire
Another way when the walls are closing in
And when I look at the space between
Where I used to be and this reckoning
I know I will never be alone

There was another in the fire
Standing next to me
There was another in the waters
Holding back the seas
And should I ever need reminding
Of how I've been set free
There is a cross that bears the burden
Where another died for me

Another In The Fire – Hillsong United

My story with the Hillsong Ministry started when I was still a preteenager, more than twenty years ago, with their album "By Your Side". The first time I watched one of their live videos, it was my cousin Maxime, always such a passionate young boy, who one day played the video at my parents' house. I believe what stood out to me at that moment was to see a young boy like Marty Sampson praising God among the elderly of his church who worship songs with such passion. Though I had not encountered Jesus yet as my Lord and Savior, I knew about Him through my mom, who was a believer. I thought it was the coolest thing I had ever seen. The praise was different from what older people used to play and what I was used to. It is the music genre that spoke to me.

In my teenage years, I was a huge pop-rock lover. Avril Lavigne, Nickelback, Kyo (a French rock band), and all those from that generation were literally my idols. I know some of my friends used to wonder how I would prefer 'white people's music' over R&B. One thing was true for me: I loved the beats and how it required little to no effort to just 'jump-dance', unlike black people's music that required dancing skills I didn't have much back then. I almost got into gothic rock, too, but it didn't take long for me to get out of that zone because something in me made me uncomfortable about all the darkness in that musical genre.

When I gave my life to Christ for the first time, I was at the end of my teenage years, and I needed to listen to Christian music I could identify with. That's when I remembered Hillsong and fully immersed myself in their ministry. Literally, that is what I was listening to the most. There were other singers like Britt Nicole, Brandon Heath, and Jeremy Camp that I loved listening to, but Hillsong Worship, I would play them everywhere I went, and I'd sing so much so that I got a good number of my friends into listening to them that today they come back and thank me for being annoying back then with my love for these Australian Christian singers. I can never be thankful enough for the impact that Darlene Zschech, Brooke Fraser, Reuben Morgan, Marty Sampson, and Joel Houston had in my walk with Christ. These people pioneered the modern worship movement in such an inspiring way.

When I was pregnant with Caleb, I used to place my headphones on my belly and play some Hillsong music with him. Sometimes, I would tell him, "You'll be a Hillsong singer one day, my son". I had always wanted my son to encounter God at a very young age and never depart from His ways, unlike me at some point in my life. Today, when I look back at Caleb's life, one thing that gives me a big smile is watching his videos of dancing to "Yes Jesus Loves Me" and "Let It Shine" from Listener Kids.

What I always found so interesting about Hillsong music was that each album had at least one song that would speak directly to a situation in my life I was going through. In the beginning, it was a lot about my fierce confession of faith in Christ. "One Way" was the song I'd play and sing as loud as my ugly voice could go. I even made a wall art in my university studio room that read "One Way, Jesus". I thought that was cool, and it was a way for me to say I was all about Jesus. When "Lead Me To The Cross" came out, your girl right here sat for a whole week creating an animated cartoon with that song. I was so proud of my cartoon video, but unfortunately, I lost it when my laptop got stolen. I didn't know much about saving my files on the cloud back then.

In 2019, when Caleb passed away, Hillsong released the album "People," and the song "Another In The Fire" hit me like I wasn't expecting. Each sentence of that song uplifted my soul and took me into a deeper revelation and outward confession of my belief in Christ right when my faith became so shaky that I thought I'd lose it.

I was in my bathroom that evening, my headphones on, and my music was playing so loud that I couldn't hear myself speaking. I used to do that a lot during that time because it was a way to numb myself from the pain and think about something other than my present reality. I couldn't cared less at that time if this act could cause harm to my hearing or not; all I wanted was the word of God through worship music to numb my pain. I would lock myself either in our bathroom or the closet and cry and praise God at the same time until I got tired of crying and singing. Where could I go? Where could I stand? What could I do to make this moment disappear? Staying in God's presence was my only medicine. I had no job and no activity I was willing to engage in, so I had a lot of time to sink into sorrow and despair. Minutes were like hours, days like months. I wanted the pain to stop at some point, but time was looking at me as if there was nothing it could do to help me. My husband was working so he could get busy with other things. I used to secretly envy him because he had an activity that would take his mind away from not having Caleb around. I can only imagine how hard it was for him not to have to drop Caleb off in the morning at the daycare and pick him up in the evening after work. That routine wasn't part of his days anymore and that must have been difficult for Michael to deal with.

At that time, I was still not done graduating from my interior design course, but I decided to stop. One of the main reasons why I got into design was because I wanted to contribute to providing a stable lifestyle for my son one day. I wanted him to be proud of the success that his mom accomplished in her design journey. Sometimes, when I was studying and doing my assignments, he would come and hang around me, and we'd cuddle and take selfies. One night, we were home just by ourselves. My husband was out of town for work. I studied very late that night, and he got tired of waiting for me to go to bed (he slept in our bed). So, he created a sleeping nest in my back with a pillow and his red blanket without me noticing and fell asleep. When I realized the noise had died down, I turned and saw my son sleeping there on the floor of the kitchen (my desk corner was in the kitchen). It was so cute I couldn't help but take a picture before closing my computer and carrying him to bed. When he passed away, there was no point anymore to continue with this long-time dream of mine. Who would I be doing it for? It was like I had no one to leave a legacy to.

I thank God today that Ornella talked me into finishing my interior design course. In memory of him, as she said, I was to finish this course. I had always admired the way she loved and cared for our son. She sometimes tells me that if our friendship were to end, I could trust that she'd always show up for any event or instance that concerned Caleb because that was her son. Six months after finishing that course, I got my first job in the US as an Online Design Specialist, which was the beginning of my career as an Interior Designer.

So, that evening, I was in front of my mirror in the bathroom watching "Another In the Fire" on YouTube for the first time. The melody was great, and the singer was new to me. For years, I had been following Hillsong, so when a new team member joined the team, I believed I'd be able to identify the newcomer. The singer, Chris Davenport, had a captivating demeanor. I had never seen him before then, or at least, I could not recognize him. As the music was going on, I started babbling the lyrics. Suddenly, after about five minutes of the song playing, there came a break in the song, and Chris Davenport, with such an assertive voice, sang, "Even if he doesn't, I will praise him. Even if he doesn't, I will stand tall", and just when I realized how powerful his declaration was, Joel Houston joined in to sing that break with him and literally screaming at this point in his microphone "I'm not bowing to this world. I ain't changing my confession or my belief or whom I believe in. Oh, I'm gonna sing louder than ever..." There it was! Hillsong once again was able to uplift and empower my soul!

Deep down inside me, before I heard the song, I had been believing and saying these words but not with enough conviction. I was too broken to speak it out loud and make sense of it. In a very shy and dubitative way, I'd say to myself that there was no way I'd leave the faith because I had experienced life without God, and it was not that great. Yet, because of how hurt and upset I was at God, I decided that I'd still serve Him but with a heavy heart. I'm telling you, when I heard these guys singing that night, at first I couldn't believe they'd sing my heart, but more than that, they empowered me in such a strong way that night that whenever the enemy would mess up with my mind from that point on, I will just scream back at him, with the strength Joel Houston had in the song "I'm not bowing to your lies. I'm not changing my confession or my belief or whom I believe in, even if He didn't resurrect my son."

Living a healthy Christian life, one marked by daily growth in the knowledge of our Lord and active work towards the realization of His kingdom, makes you a prime target for the enemy's attacks, who hopes to defeat you. To effectively counter such assaults, you need a profound understanding of the God you serve. Without growth in your faith, you'll find yourself easily overwhelmed when challenges arise. The enemy focuses his efforts not on the lukewarm believer, but on those who pose a genuine threat to his plans.

When my son passed away, I experienced firsthand one of the enemy's tactics: an assault on my mind. He sowed seeds of doubt about God's love for me and my family, reminiscent of his deception of Eve in the Garden of Eden. This is, in essence, the root of sin – the cultivation of doubt and disbelief.

From my study of the interaction between the serpent and the woman, leading to the original sin that got us into being separated from God, I noticed three steps it took for sin to be conceived.

1. ***The enemy will make you doubt God's word.***

   In Genesis 3:1 (NIV), he starts by telling Eve, "Did God really say you must not eat the fruit from any of the trees in the garden?" The truth is, yes, he really did say it. Eve says in Genesis 3:2-3 (NIV), "Of course, we may eat fruit from the trees in the garden. It's only the fruit from the tree in the middle of the garden that we are not allowed to eat. God said, 'You must not eat it or even touch it; if you do, you will die.'"

   Though she knew the word, and because we know how all this ended, we can agree that he succeeded in leaving her questioning something she knew deep down was true.

2. ***The enemy deceives you by making you believe God is hiding something from you.***

He continues to say in Genesis 3:5 (NIV), "God knows that your eyes will be opened as soon as you eat it, and you will be like God, knowing both good and evil."

I believe the enemy wanted Eve to see God in a way that He wasn't. He wanted to distort God's image in her sight by lying about God's real intentions.

3. ***We're filled with lust and envy, and then we allow ourselves to fall.***

It says in Genesis 3:6 (NIV): The woman was convinced. She saw that the tree was beautiful, and its fruit looked delicious, and she wanted the wisdom it would give her. So, she took some of the fruit and ate it. Then she gave some to her husband, who was with her, and he ate it, too.

At this point, she probably started picturing what it would be like to be like God, and that surely pleased her, and before we knew it, sin happened.

More than once, I had the enemy making me doubt God's love for me and my family. "If God really did love you, he won't take Caleb away." "You see how you've been faithfully serving God these past years, and yet he took your only one." These are some of the things he'll whisper to my mind. I mean, I was in pain, grieving, and yet he won't stop punching me. Because yes, those were punches. The enemy has no pity, no remorse, and no compassion. It is just crazy to think about how deep and strong his wickedness can go. Basically, what he wanted was for me to deny my faith. I must be honest; so many times, I wanted to do it, but deep down, I knew the world didn't have something better to offer. When you find yourself in a situation like the one in which my husband and I were, that is, losing a child – what is considered unnatural (parents should never bury their kids, they say) – you don't know what to do, what to think or what to believe.

In 2017, I came back to the house of the Lord, and the first thing God taught me about Himself was "His Love". I knew, though I was in pain that I was still loved by Him. My knowledge of God's love for me and my loved ones was grounded. Knowing that kept me fighting back against the enemy when he would punch me. I might be down and doubting for an hour, but I'll fight back and say, "I will still serve God because I know he loves me, even if it doesn't feel like it." I have experienced life without Christ and life with Christ at the core center of my life, and nothing beats being led fully and intentionally by God.

So, even if He didn't spare Caleb's life that day, even if He didn't spare my husband and me from the pain of losing a child, even if He didn't allow us to raise Caleb from the dead (because yes, He could do it as He did for Lazarus John 11:43-44 (NIV)) and gave us His power to perform miracles as well Mark 16:17-18 (NIV)), even if He didn't do all those things, my confession will not change, my belief will remain unshaken, for I know He loves my family and me more than I can even fathom to imagine.

HOLY SPIRIT, MY BEST FRIEND

Holy Spirit I bless You

Holy Spirit I honor You

Holy Spirit I love You

You are my best friend

You are my comforter

You are my strength

You are my helper

I ask you Holy Spirit

Take me into the deep things of God

Take me into the revelation of the Father

And the revelation of the Son

Holy Spirit I just tell you right now, thank you

Thank you that you have taken up residence on the inside of me

You will never leave me nor forsake me

You are the burning fire in my spirit

You are the rushing river in my spirit

You are the glory in my spirit and you shine

Holy Spirit – Corey Russell

One of my close friends, Keira, who also was my productivity and business coach, once told me, "Sometimes, before your physical body gets into doing something, your spirit whispered it to you months or years ago, but at that time, you didn't even know what those thoughts meant until your physical body grasped it". I mean, if that isn't a true statement, then I don't know!!!

Here's a little story about my friend: We went to the same youth church in Cameroon (the same church Martha attended as well). I've always admired how uncompromising and authentic she feared and loved God. In my business, as much as I can, I try to be intentional about the people I work with. And Keira is one of those women I've always enjoyed working with. At almost every working session, she'd pray for me and make powerful declarations about my life and my career. We understand that what we do is, first and foremost, for the kingdom of God. We use our talents for His glory, and we enjoy doing business that way.

On my birthday, June 4, 2018, two days after I got married to Michael, I was in my bed talking to my cousin, Viviane. She is the firstborn of my generation on my mom's side and a very good friend of mine. I remember telling God while being on the phone with her, "Now I'm ready for the next challenge, but not death, God". I giggled, and she told me, before thinking about the next challenge, to enjoy this victory God had won for me. She was talking about how God changed Michael's heart about never wanting to remarry to who he was now, my husband!

But why would my mouth say "not death" that day? Of all the different types of challenges life can offer, why and how was I able to mention death?

A month after our wedding, we, with Caleb, were on the way to the airport to pick up my sister-friend Jessica. We've known each other since we were 9 and 11 years old, and she was one of those women I trusted with my son's life. She loved and cared for Caleb as if he was hers. She was coming from Cameroon to spend time with us in Houston. On our way there, I was having a text conversation with Martha that led me to say, "If Michael and Caleb ever find themselves in a deadly car accident and I'm asked to choose who should survive, I will choose Michael". My sentence choked the hell out of my friend. As thoughtful, polite, and Holy-Spirit filled as she was, she asked me why I'd say that because she couldn't believe a parent, moreover a mom, would say that. In her logic, a mom will always choose her child over her partner.

Mind you, at that moment, I wasn't on very good terms with my husband, so logically, I'd have chosen my son over my husband, right? Well, I stood firmly on my words and belief, and this is what I told her: "If Caleb dies today, I have the firm assurance that he is going to heaven, but if Michael dies now without accepting Jesus in his life as Lord and Savior, his soul will forever be separated from God. So as crazy as I sound, I will choose that Michael lives because that gives him an opportunity on earth to confess Jesus".

I loved my son like crazy. He was my cuddling partner. He was my mini-me. He was my "petit papa" because he had my dad's name, Toby. He was my joy and my pride. He was smart and handsome, like his dad. He was stylish. He was funny. He was strong-willed, and he was oh-so-loving, like me. If you knew me when Caleb was alive, you'd testify of my attachment towards him. Despite it all, I never stopped asking God to show my son how to love Him, God, more than he loved me and his dad, and I'd ask God to help me never make my love for Caleb bigger than my love for Him, God. I didn't want to be the type of parent who would turn my child into a god, and I didn't want my child to turn his parents into gods. My desire was and still is to see my family serve and love Yahweh first and above everything else.

I was able to voice out those words to Martha because my spirit, as Keira told me, was in advance of my reality. It knew about the things to come, and because it did, it started preparing me in my actions, declarations, and thoughts to be able to conquer the waves when the storm hit. I didn't know it at that time, but the Holy Spirit prepared me for the toughest moment of my life.

Sometimes, I thought after Caleb left that I wish I didn't say those things, that I didn't pray those prayers, that I didn't think that way, but the thing is, I cannot own one hundred percent of those thoughts, and words because the Holy Spirit spoke about the things to come to my spirit, through my words and understanding. But even though it wasn't fully from mine, I believe that the Holy Spirit will only impact the way you think or speak if He finds fertile ground. That is a heart that is willing to serve God truly and sincerely. I was in no way manipulated nor in trans. I was aware of what I said, but I had no idea, not even in my darkest nightmares, that I was speaking about the future. But again, God can only use you for His glory if you let yourself be used by Him, and this is a willful and conscious decision.

Therefore, I urge you, brothers and sisters, in view of God's mercy, to offer your bodies as a living sacrifice, holy and pleasing to God—this is your true and proper worship. Romans 12:1 [NIV]

No matter how scary living this life as a believer in Jesus Christ can be, my deepest desire will always be to be used in any possible way by God. And without the Holy Spirit (HS), my life as a believer in Jesus Christ will make no sense. Everything that I am and do good, I owe it to the Holy Spirit. He walks this life with me. He fills me up with His joy. He advises me when I need to make decisions (even though I don't always do as He says, blaming it on my stubbornness). He teaches me how to self-control, how to be grateful, how to speak kindly, how to love, and how to be compassionate and gentle. If you know me personally and there are things about me that you truly appreciate, know that the Holy Spirit is behind every good action that I take.

And I will pray to the Father, and he shall give you another Comforter, that he may abide with you forever. John 14:13 [KJV]

The morning Jesus visited me, I was crying and asking Him where He was when Caleb passed away; I remember He showed me the Holy Spirit, laying His hands on my shoulders and breathing strength in me. During that season of deep sorrow, the Holy Spirit was the one comforting me. He was compassionate towards me. He was the only one to understand me. What I write might sound crazy or stupid, but if you've never experienced who the Holy Spirit is, then you'd not know how important of a person He can be in your life. The Holy Spirit, I call Him my best friend. He calls me beautiful. He doesn't sugarcoat the truth to me. He rebukes me when I'm acting stupid. He reminds me of the scriptures and gives me the wisdom to act right. If not for Him, I would not have been able to stand today and write this book.

In 2007, when I gave my life to Christ, it all started with Him. Like I jokingly say, "he knocked me down like a strong wind and came to dwell in me". When I came back to the house of the Lord for the second – and final – time in 2016, I knew He'd never leave. When Caleb passed, I knew he was always there. I never questioned that because, unfailingly, He has been walking with me and preparing me for this moment. That's why when I asked Jesus where He was when Caleb left, I didn't address the Holy Spirit directly because I've always been convinced of His presence in my everyday life. Strangely, it is also in this season that I learned how to clearly distinguish the voice of the Holy Spirit, that of Jesus the Son, and that of Abba Father. I'm sure you're probably wondering how that is possible, but it is a mystery to me as well. Yes, they're inseparable; that is the trinity. Yet it is three persons in one God. In my understanding, they're equally God, but they don't have the same function. Therefore, they don't speak the same, understand, not have the same voice, but they're in accord and speak about the same things.

I remember how every single time I didn't have the strength to pray, I'd go into the closet and just cry out, "Holy Spirit, I am hurting, and I don't know how to do this. Help me". For hours, I'd cry, and I knew my best friend was there with me. I'm telling you, some scriptures will only make sense when you go through certain experiences. When the Bible says in Romans 8:26, *"In the same way, the Spirit helps us in our weaknesses. We do not know what we ought to pray for, but the Spirit himself intercedes for us through wordless groans"*, it is true.

For you to have a healthy relationship with the Holy Spirit, there are three fundamental questions I believe you need to ask yourself. These are:

- Who is the Holy Spirit?

- What exactly does He do?

- How do you receive Him?

I'll take you through my personal experience to answer these questions:

1. *Who is the Holy Spirit?*

Now the earth was formless and empty, darkness was over the surface of the deep, and the Spirit of God was hovering over the waters. Genesis 1:2 [NIV]

Way before Jesus' ministry on earth came to pass and gave us the promise of sending the Holy Spirit, the Holy Spirit already existed and roamed on earth. He is not a new concept. He is not even a concept or a thing. The Holy Spirit is a person. He is the Spirit of God. He is the third person of the Trinity, and He is the one who sustains us today as believers to be able to walk this Christian life. Some believers describe Him as that small voice inside of you that directs you to the right path. I call Him my best friend.

2. *What exactly does He do?*

And I will ask the Father, and he will give you another advocate to help you and be with you forever – the Spirit of truth. The world cannot accept him because it neither sees him nor knows him. But you know him, for he lives with you and will be in you. – John 14:16-17 [NIV]

There are so many things the Holy Spirit can do in your life. I urge you to get into the scriptures and discover for yourself the depth of his ministry. I'd say this: The HS will and can be anything you let Him be in your life. For the sake of this book, I'll take you through who He has been for me during the season Caleb recently left.

- He was my teacher. He'd show me how to deal with my emotions regarding Caleb's departure and how to handle some of the negative energy I was getting from my husband. I was going through a lot in my marriage, and at that time, the Holy Spirit showed up, teaching me how to be self-controlled, patient, and compassionate towards Michael.

- He was my counselor. Like a therapist, He'd advise me on how to move on, how to dig deeper and ask myself tough questions, leading to me knowing and understanding the reasons for some of my actions and that of my husband at that time.

- He was my consoler. I loved how He'd reassure me that crying was okay; I didn't have to be strong when I couldn't. And every time it would happen that I cried, He would be there next to me, collecting my tears.

- He was like my guardian angel. He used loved ones and even strangers around me to remind me that He watches over my steps and even provides for my smallest needs.

- He was my best friend. Sometimes, when I'm home just by myself cooking, together we'll be cracking silly jokes, and I'll burst out laughing. When I tell you God has a sense of humor, believe me, it is true. I never felt lonely with Him by my side.

- He was my love. There is nothing He does out of love. His actions towards me are rooted in His unconditional and unfailing love for me.

3. *How do you receive him?*

Jesus answered, *"Very truly I tell you, no one can enter the kingdom of God unless they are born of water and the Spirit. Flesh gives birth to flesh, but the Spirit gives birth to spirit. You should not be surprised at my saying, 'You must be born again.'* John 3:5-7 [NIV]

Receiving the Holy Spirit in your life is about accepting Jesus as your Lord and Savior. Acknowledging that His life on earth and His ministry were true. His unconditional love for you is available for you to accept as a gift. Once you wholeheartedly make Jesus Lord over your life, you instantly receive the Holy Spirit inside of you. And once you have the Holy Spirit in you, His power in you needs to be activated. It's like buying a toy. When you buy it, you bring it to your house, and it's yours for you to keep. For it to function, you must press the ON button. You decide to do so. The same goes with the Holy Spirit. He'll fully be active in your life if you let Him be.

Knowing the Holy Spirit is more than praying in tongues. Knowing the HS is about creating a relationship with Him. It's about trusting Him when He says, "Don't do it, don't go there", because He knows it all and has your best interest at heart. Being a believer and faithfully walking with the Holy Spirit is a plus that nothing in this world can offer. I'll forever be grateful to God for the gift of His Spirit.

GOD IS GOOD

I love You, Lord

For Your mercy never fails me

All my days, I've been held in Your hands

From the moment that I wake up

Until I lay my head

Oh, I will sing of the goodness of God

Cause all my life you have been faithful

And all my life you have been so, so good

With every breath that I am able

Oh, I will sing of the goodness of God

Goodness of God – Bethel Music

"God is good, all the time; And all the time, God is good." I'm sure you heard this saying somewhere, in church, at a Christian concert, or from the mouth of someone you know. But let me ask you this: do you really believe it? If you've once said it yourself, have you ever sat down and known exactly why you say it and believe it or not?

In my journey with Christ, I've realized that each challenge reveals a new aspect of who God is. Before my son Caleb's passing, God demonstrated His nature as love and His ability to transform hearts. This understanding began in my first year in the US, when the Holy Spirit taught me about God's perfect love, even amidst my mistakes, before I made my confession of faith. A significant moment of transformation was when God changed Michael's heart about remarrying.

Recognizing God's love was essential before I faced the unimaginable challenge of losing my only son. I understood that without a firm belief in God's love, the forthcoming season of my life would be even more difficult to navigate.

Despite feeling hurt, crushed, and devastated to the point of contemplating suicide, I chose to mourn in communion with the Lord. I cried out, 'Why me, Lord? Why now? Why?' Even with my knowledge of His love, I couldn't help but question His affection during those dark moments. This loss led me to deeply question many aspects of my faith and life.

Who did God, therefore, become to me amid my grief and sorrow? What new aspect of Him did He want me to see or experience?

Well, God became the 'Good Father' to me. How can God be good in such circumstances, you'd ask, right? At some point, I knew I'd be asked to answer that question, so I started journaling about it and diving deeper into His word to see how He had shown goodness to His people during sorrow.

How do you explain God's goodness amid sorrow? How do you see it? How do you feel or experience it? The first thing you need to know is God's goodness has nothing to do with the situation you are going through. God being good is about His fundamental nature as our Abba father. In the good times, He is good. In the bad times, He is also good.

To me, when I say God is good, it's like I'm talking about a design package that contains different deliverables. "Goodness" is the package character of God, and in it are His character attributes I called earlier deliverables. The attributes I was able to experience were care, provision, love, kindness, patience, and presence.

For you to understand better how good God was to me amid sorrow, I'll share stories and instances where I was able to experience these characteristics that make Him a 'Good Good Father'.

1. Care

See how very much our father loves us, for he calls us his children, and that is what we are! But the people who belong to this world don't recognize that we are God's children because they don't know him. 1 John 3:1 [NLT]

As a parent, one of the things you care the most about is knowing that your children are safe and taken care of. When God took my son, that was Him reassuring me that my son was in good hands. I'm living my life today having the firm assurance of where my son is. He is safe from the aches of this world. He's safe from ever losing his soul to the enemy. This is God's goodness to me. "I'm taking care of him, so don't worry about him anymore," He told me. What God has done for me as His child was to show me love beyond measure. That same love is available to anyone who believes and sees Him as Abba Father.

2. *Provision*

Abraham named the place Yahweh-Yireh (which means "the Lord will provide"). To this day, people still use that name as a proverb: "On the mountain of the Lord it will be provided." Genesis 22:14 [NLT]

Sometimes, when we think about provision, what comes to mind is tangible things like food, clothes, money, etc. I have found, however, that the most meaningful things God provides for me are things I can't physically hold, like joy, peace, opportunities, and even the Holy Spirit. During my early grieving period, God provided me with a community of people who showed us love and prayed for us, from my church community at New Life Church in Houston to our family members and friends around the world. The support was more than we could ever imagine receiving.

3. *Love*

There is no fear in love, but perfect love drives out fear because fear involves punishment, and the one who fears is not perfected in love. 1 John 4:18 [NASB]

I was raised in a culture where questioning the person in charge (the authority) was simply not acceptable. I have always struggled with it because God made me a 'why-child,' and that isn't always easy. I question, not because I want to disagree, but because I need to understand the reasoning to adjust accordingly.

In my walk with Christ, after the Holy Spirit taught me about God's love, He has allowed me to confidently ask Him tough questions about the scripture and anything in between. So, whenever I have a question, I don't hesitate to go before Him without fear of judgment because I know He loves me.

On April 05, 2019, almost a month after Caleb passed away. I was in tears, thinking in my heart that this God might be selfish sometimes. I couldn't help it anymore; I screamed: "Why does everything always have to be about YOUR glory?" He kindly replied: "Why do you love me?"

When the Lord asked me why I loved Him, I swear, I instantly shushed, wiped my tears away, and got into a super silent mode with an open heart. Sometimes, when I ask God some questions, He won't always directly give me the answer because He wants me to dig deeper and come up with reasonable answers by myself. This has helped me develop my critical thinking. In my silent moment, I came to understand three fundamental truths about God's glory.

- Regardless of how I feel about a situation, God deserves the glory because He is God. Period! There are countless reasons for Him to be praised. He gave me a breath of life. He made me walk, talk, see, and taste. He created the heavens, the earth, and everything inside. And even if I don't feel like giving Him praise, He's more than capable of making the stones cry out to Him because He is God (Revelation 4:11).

- My mom is a genuine human being. She's the type who will turn a servant into a child. I have seen her do things for people who didn't even deserve her love. Yet, she'll wholeheartedly do it over again and never let pride fill her heart. In acting that way, I can't help but praise my mom. Remember that pride is attached to selfishness, and selfishness is about oneself only. It is because my mom exerts the character of Christ that I'm able to see God through her. And if this is how God looks like, why then would I ever have a problem directly giving God the glory when what I see in my mom is God? In other words, if I'm able to praise my mom for good deeds, why shouldn't I praise God, the author of the good deeds He operates through her? Truly, He's worthy of all my praise (Ephesians 5:1)

- This last point is my favorite to back up God's selflessness regarding my questioning. The Bible says in Romans 8:17-18 [TPT] that *"And since we are his true children, we qualify to share all his treasures, for indeed, we are heirs of God himself. And since we are joined to Christ, we also inherit all that he is and all that he has. We will experience being co-glorified with him, provided that we accept his sufferings as our own. I am convinced that any suffering we endure is less than nothing compared to the magnitude of glory that is to be unveiled within us"*. Do I need to add anything more?

4. *Kindness*

In a surge of anger, I hid my face from you for a moment, but with everlasting kindness, I will have compassion on you," says the Lord your Redeemer. Isaiah 54:8 [NIV]

Every time I think about God's kindness towards me, it is first that feeling of undeserved compassion that will come to my mind. Kindness is like a chain of action. When someone does something good to you, you want to give back in return. When God gave me Caleb after my abortion, I saw it as God being kind to me despite my previous mistakes. More than being compassionate, I see His kindness through the friendly and soft way the Holy Spirit sometimes interacts with me. I know that no matter what, I'll always experience His caring hands over me.

5. *Patience*

For my name's sake, I defer my anger, and for the sake of my praise, I restrain it for you, that I may not cut you off. Isaiah 48:9 [NIV]

One time, I had a conversation with a friend, to whom I was explaining that we're no different from the Israelites wandering 40 years in the desert. We find ourselves falling into the same mistakes repeatedly because of our stubbornness, yet God will still be there to rescue us and not give up on us till one day we're mature enough to abandon our bad ways for good. It took me about six years to come back to the house of the Lord as a prodigal. During that entire time, God patiently never left my side until I came back home. If this is not goodness, then I don't know what it is.

6. *Presence*

If your heart is broken, you'll find God right there if you're kicked in the gut. He'll help you catch your breath. Psalm 34:8 [MSG]

God uses humans to operate in humans' lives. As much as it is true in the spiritual realm that He is present by our sides, it is also true physically through human intervention. I remember that afternoon when I decided to jump off my balcony because I couldn't take it anymore. Suicide was best; I believed the enemy's lie. On my way to my balcony, I received a call from my cousin in Cameroon. "Coco, how are you handling things today?" she asked. I burst out, "Viviane, I want to die". I won't stop crying. With the scriptures, she was able to calm me down, and my suicide mission was aborted. Around the same time, one afternoon, I was in my chair in my bedroom, crying so hard that I could feel like my heart would crush, literally. The pain was excruciating, and I wished death over me. Suddenly, I received a call from Pastor Hughes, my youth pastor in

Cameroon, and once again, with scriptures, he calmed me down. I spent the rest of that day singing and dancing to worship music. Then there was this time, still in a moment of extreme sorrow when my heart felt the same crushing pain; I received a call from a friend, Sidonie. She prayed for me, spoke the word of God over me, and at the end of that week or the following, came to pick me up to spend the weekend with her and her family. Altogether, it happened about six times where I was in such deep sadness that it felt like my chest was crushing my heart, literally, and I wished to die at those exact moments. All those times, I had either a call or a text, whose goals were specific – to display God's presence to my broken heart.

This is what God's goodness looked like to me. When I was in the closet crying, He was crying with me. When I wanted to vent, his loving patience was my shield. When I felt lonely in my sorrow, He provided a community. When I was hopeless, He reminded me of His promises. He never left my side. He was genuinely kind and soft-spoken to me. Words can't explain the assurance that I have in knowing that God is good!

MY ONLY SON, BUT WHY?

For God so loved the word

That He gave His only Son

And whosoever believes will not perish

They shall have eternal life

God So Loved – Hillsong Worship

Caleb's birth provided me the opportunity to be a mother and experience God's grace and forgiveness following my abortion. However, his impact on my life extended beyond this. I refer to it as 'ministry' because I believe every Christ follower is, in essence, a minister. This means that as believers, irrespective of our professions – be it teaching, designing, engineering, or others – we each have a ministry grounded in our general purpose: to know God personally and make Him known to others.

The Bible teaches that God knew us before our birth (Jeremiah 1:5) and is aware of the plans He has for us, including the number of our days (Psalm 139:16). Yet, it acknowledges that premature deaths can occur due to our actions (Ecclesiastes 7:17). This understanding compels me to regularly declare a life of abundance for myself and my loved ones, echoing my mother's words: "I stand against every premature death in the name of Jesus!" These declarations are a conscious part of my life. However, we must remember that nothing surprises God. Caleb's final day on earth was ordained; to us, it was an unexpected and unwelcome surprise.

I was born in the church, but I didn't care much about the church. I would go because my mom and her sisters would go and because I loved that we were always so nicely dressed on Sunday, and I wouldn't miss an opportunity to show off my pretty outfits or my sense of style. I haven't changed much on that one. I love fashion and style, and inevitably, I got it from my mom and her sisters. So very early, I heard about Jesus, but I didn't know Him personally. I can even go to the extent of saying that I didn't care much about the fact that God gave his only son for the sake of mankind. What would I even know about having a child at that age? Moreover, having only one child?

It was in the summer of 2007, during a youth camp organized by my church, that I was born again and had a better understanding of how God loved me and mankind. Little did I know at the time that a deeper revelation of His sacrifice would come to me as He would let me go through a tragedy that would forever change my life on earth.

I was in my bedroom one afternoon, and I was praying and most certainly crying. I didn't have a job back then, and I stopped attending my interior design course. I felt like my life was meaningless and purposeless. I felt so lonely and sad. I wouldn't stop talking to God because I knew the only one who would understand my pain was Him. So, I spent hours talking to Him audibly, in my heart, in my journal and often fell asleep in my tears. Right after Caleb's funeral in April 2019, the Lord asked me to take some time off from social media. That was the very first time I got into 'social media fasting', which is something I still practice whenever I want to focus on God and get away from distractions.

Ever since Caleb left, I had not stopped asking God, "Why Caleb? Why me? Why now?" I couldn't wrap my brain around the fact that a God who by now had become my best friend would let that happen to me. I needed closure to be able to move on, and I thought the best closure was to know why. The more I asked, the more I felt His silence. I was so angry, hurt, and disappointed that I couldn't see beyond my pain. One time, I remembered screaming at God, "How could you do that to me? I was your best friend! I was talking with you every day. I was sharing with you every detail of my life. Why would you do that to me? Why would you take me to a foreign country and take away from me the only thing that made me happy? What did I do wrong? Why would you punish me, Lord? Why?" It felt like a friend had stabbed me in my back, and my brain couldn't process it. I was in such pain that I wanted to open my chest and take my heart out of it. In those moments, I admired Jeremy Camp's courage and willingness to move on without ever having an answer from God as to why He allowed his first wife to die from cancer.

Being alone with God during that social media fasting time, without anybody calling or texting me, my mind started shifting away from my desperate need to know why God took Caleb. I started reminding myself that though God let it happen, His love for me was still very real. He loved Caleb as much, and if He wanted to, He would not have let him go, but He had a plan. God has always known me to be his 'why-daughter', the one who will ask questions that no one asks or cares to ask, so it was certainly no surprise to Him to hear me harass Him with my 'whys'. In my questioning process, what I needed to understand and acknowledge was that God didn't owe me any answer, and that's because He is God. If He was to answer all my whys, then He won't be God anymore. I also needed to understand that sometimes God will not answer because I might not be spiritually ready yet to handle the answer the right way. Gradually, in my mind, I started accepting that it was okay for me never to have an answer to why He took Caleb. Little did I know that my surrender would yield a revelation. So, seated in the corner chair of my bedroom that afternoon, I made this heartfelt prayer: "Lord, I know you love me, and I know you loved Caleb too. I know you had our best interest at heart, and whatever reason you took Caleb for, I'll not only trust that it's for our good, but I pray that your purpose comes to completion..." I wasn't done praying when I heard in my spirit, "I took Caleb so that I could have Michael's attention and for him to be saved, just as you were." I couldn't believe what I heard! At the same time, I knew this wasn't something my brain could have formulated because it made no sense to me! Abruptly, I stopped the prayer, fell on my knees, and to the top of my lungs, I screamed, "LORD! THE PRICE WAS TOO HIGH!" and I broke down in tears.

I was inconsolable. All types of thoughts and questions were going through my mind. First, I was in shock that God told me why He took Caleb. Second, I couldn't understand how far God would go for the sake of salvation. But again, isn't He who says He will leave the ninety-nine and run for that one lost sheep (Matthew 18:12-13)? As I was there lying on the floor crying, I realized how much God loved my husband, Michael. Truth be told, I wasn't very happy about God's plan. For a very long time now, my relationship with Michael was unstable and filled with so many wounds that some part of me grew cold towards him. I couldn't help but wonder if he even deserved that much of God's attention and love. So, for the remaining days of my fasting season, I asked God to fill my heart with a deeper love for Michael's soul. Ever since, I have not stopped faithfully praying for my husband to come back to the house of the Lord, just like I once did that night, staring at my son in his crib when God spoke to me about His love for me.

"For God so loved the world that he gave his one and only Son, that whoever believes in him shall not perish but have eternal life." (John 3:16). This is probably the first scripture I had to memorize, as a child who grew up in the church. It was a foundational scripture to our faith, and though we might not have known the depth of what it meant at that young age, my Sunday school teachers made it a priority for us to know that God's love for mankind was so deep that He would sacrifice the only child He had, for our salvation. When I was finally able to calm down, I told God that afternoon that, truly, the price was too high because that was my only son. He replied, "Now you have a better understanding of how I feel about people despising my only son's sacrifice." It broke my heart. Sometimes, we tend to think that Abba's father doesn't have feelings, but I don't believe it to be true. If God is capable of loving, getting angry, and being jealous, then yes, I do believe I serve a God that has feelings. Abba Father sacrificed His only son so that we can be saved and live eternity in His presence and not away from Him. Every single day

that we get up, we can acknowledge and experience Jesus' love and sacrifice for us.

When Jesus came to this earth in human form, He came to reconcile us to God the Father. The original sin of Adam and Eve separated us from the Father, and humanity needed a savior, so Jesus paid that price on the cross. Jesus brought a message of love, compassion, and forgiveness. He taught us how to love and please the Father and how to love and interact with one another. Yet He was despised and rejected by mankind, a man of suffering and familiar with pain. *Like one from whom people hide their faces, he was despised, and we held him in low esteem.* (Isaiah 53:3 NIV). You tell me, as a parent, if your child was to solely take the blame for their friends, for those same friends again to spit and reject them, how would you feel? What would you do? Just imagine that child of yours wasn't even your only one; he had siblings. Won't you still feel crushed and hurt? Now imagine that child of yours was your one and only child, who didn't just stop at taking the blame but went right to die for the sake of their ungrateful friends; how would you feel?

When I lost my one and only son, I understood the heart of God. It's a painful place to be, but God, in His abundant love and patience, is still 'begging' us to consider His son's sacrifice. He doesn't stop pursuing us. He uses other believers to bring more believers to the house – to Know God and make Him know, right? Becoming a child of God is a choice you make. Let me write that again: it is a choice! To be born again, not of the flesh but of the spirit (John 3:1-15) is to believe and accept Jesus in your life as Lord and Savior. I did it; many others did it. If you've never done it, I pray one day you come to join this amazing family of God. This is the best decision you can ever take for your life now and for your eternity; that is life after physical death. God loves you more than you could ever imagine. He sacrificed His only son, Jesus Christ so that you could enjoy a close relationship with Him, Abba Father, and experience the beauty of living this life on earth with the Holy Spirit till Jesus' return. God desperately wants us to come back home to Him and turn away from our wrongdoing. That's why it took Him to let His only son be sacrificed for our sake. He will not let His children get lost (Matthew 18:14). He'll do everything possible to get back your attention.

God used Caleb's life to minister to me, and I see how He is still using him, though he's not with us anymore. Some people will come into your life to accomplish a specific purpose and leave. Caleb came into my life to make me understand God's love for me. I shared with you, in chapter four, the story of my 'second salvation' and how my son played a significant role in it. Even though my son was conceived in sin, the entire situation didn't stop God from doing what He wanted to accomplish. With God, no situation is too desperate or too dirty for Him not to be able to work with. Caleb opened the doors to the United States for me, which is the land where God called me to start building the purpose He has for me. I gave you all the details about my immigration story. Moreover, I've always felt like if Michael and I didn't have a child together, I don't think he would have suggested for all of us to move to the US, and that was because we were more of Caleb's parents than we were a couple. An elderly man back home once told me that "Americans never leave their children behind, unlike Frenchs." I do not know if it's true, but that's what I was told.

Through my journey of being Caleb's mom, the Holy Spirit taught me His ways through Caleb's progression. Like that time when Caleb did something wrong, and I screamed at him for him to come and cry in my arms. At that moment, I remembered the Lord telling me this is what He wants me to do as His daughter. When I mess up, though He'll be upset at me, He wants me to come to Him with my sin so that He can fix it, rather than me turning and going away. That's why today, no matter how dirty my transgression might look, I will go to God first and tell Him I messed up. He knows that, of course, but He likes it more when I trust that His love for me is big enough to forgive me and show me how to do better the next time. There is this other lesson I learned about God giving us the room to figure things out as we mature as believers. When Caleb falls, I'll silently watch from afar to see how he'll manage to get up. If it took longer than what I was expecting from him, then I'll rush to his rescue. The observation time before the rescue time always depended on his age. When he was a baby, as soon as he fell, I'd pick him up immediately and console him. As he was getting bigger, I'd give room for him to figure things out. The Holy Spirit made me understand that He does the same with us. That's why when we're newly born again, it's like our prayers are being answered immediately. We enjoy the spiritual breastmilk. But as we grow older in our faith, prayers aren't answered as quickly, and tests and trials are introduced in our journey as believers. It's a natural progression in life. These are some of the fruits of Caleb's ministry in my life.

Just when I believed I was a done deal, God graciously let me conceive a son, through which I was brought back to the house of the Lord. His departure, more than just for Michael's salvation, has a greater impact than what I might know now. If you're able to identify with my story, then perhaps God also had you in mind concerning Caleb. The Bible says in John 7:38 that whoever believes in Him, rivers of living water will flow from within them. I had to believe and be filled so that I could pour in return. It's like a chain; we received the revelation of salvation so that we could, in turn, give it out to others.

YOUR FAITH WILL SAVE YOU

You call me out upon the waters
The great unknown where feet may fail
And there I find You in the mystery
In oceans deep my faith will stand

And I will call upon your name
And keep my eyes above the waves
When oceans rise
My soul will rest in your embrace
For I am yours and You are mine

Oceans – Hillsong United

The circumstances of Caleb's death have always been evidence to Michael, me, and some loved ones that this was a medical malpractice. And because he was under five years old, an autopsy is mandatory to establish a cause of death. We waited about a month or so for the results to come before deciding on when Caleb would be buried. The waiting time was very difficult. We were expecting some type of justice to be made at that point. Our son had never been sick before then, so it was normal for them to see no trace of sickness. The results came out, and pretty much it showed he was a healthy child whose cause of death was a heart attack. But then it left us with the question, "What caused the heart attack?" We never had an answer, even when we went right up to the point of hiring lawyers because we wanted to sue that urgent care for malpractice. To our greatest despair, our case never saw through. I can still remember March 2020 when Michael called me. I was in Cameroon for vacation, and he told me that the lawyers dropped our case. It broke our hearts. After waiting for a full year, nothing will happen. No matter how tough that decision was, I let God heal my heart because only He could help me see things from His perspective – "I let it happen."

So, one month after the autopsy, we scheduled for Caleb to be buried. The funeral home requested for us to choose his outfit and send it over, as well as a picture they'd use for the memorial card. By then, we had been living in the US for about a year and a half, and I had no intimate friends around I trusted to take me to the mall to buy my son his burial clothes. I wished Fabiola was there, but the drive from Austin to Houston just to buy clothes wasn't worth it, I thought. The same stores I used to buy his outfits at; this time, it will feel so strange. I imagined coming across kids at the store, and I wasn't sure how that would make me feel. My mom knew how sad I was and took it upon herself to reach out to one of her friends, Beatrice, in Houston to support me in this moment. Initially, my mom was supposed to come to the US during this grieving time, but she didn't have her visa and therefore couldn't make it.

I used to have a lot of prejudices about being part of Cameroonian communities because someone – a Cameroonian – I randomly met through a friend told me to avoid them, and I religiously followed this person's counsel. I didn't know any better at that time. I was relatively new in the US, and I could only follow the advice of someone who had been there way longer than I had. You can say that was a little unwise of me; I should have made my own opinion, and you're right. Today, I'm relatively immersed in my Cameroonian community, and I'm glad I am. I know how to set boundaries for myself, and I know what to share and not share or let in and not let in. So, one afternoon, Mama Beatrice – that's what I call her – called me, and we arranged to see each other the following Sunday. It was such a pleasant surprise to spend time with her. It was like I've always known her. She was so motherly, so kind. From then till today, she has become my 'Cameroonian Mommy' figure in the US. We had lunch that day, then went to the mall and I think we just bought a white shirt or black jeans, I can't remember. I completed the rest of his outfit from what he already owned at home. There was no point for me to spend too much money on something that would decay – I like to believe I do make smart decisions sometimes with my money.

In the meantime, Jessica was preparing to come to the US for Caleb's funeral. She had visited us the previous year when Caleb was still with us, and now she was returning under vastly different circumstances. I have always been profoundly grateful and honored by her willingness to support my family and me in this way. Her presence was a tangible reminder of the love and support from my loved ones back in Cameroon.

The evening before the funeral, Jessica, Michael, and I arrived in Lake Charles, Louisiana. We met with my mother-in-law and her husband and tried to relax in anticipation of the next day. We took Jessica to the Golden Nugget and L'Auberge for drinks and dinner. The following day, the day of the funeral, arrived all too soon. I woke up feeling incredibly nervous and shaky, almost to the point of fainting. Michael prepared himself early and left for the funeral home to see Caleb's body and ensure that everything was in order. His departure gave Jessica and me some additional time to get ready.

We both dressed elegantly in our black dresses and veil mesh hats I got for her, Fabiola, and myself. I was determined not to let mourning prevent me from being stylish – a tribute to my son who had always been fashion-conscious. It was a small way I could honor his memory, reflecting a passion we both shared. After ensuring everything was in place, Michael returned to pick us up.

At the funeral home, I refused to see Caleb's body. I stood by the door, and from afar, I could see his forehead from behind. It seemed darker than usual, and that was an additional sign for me that I didn't want to see that. I wanted to remember my beautiful, light-skinned son. I needed that memory to stay in me forever – by then, I still had the memory of him pinkish and lying dead in that hospital bed with some splashes of blood on his face. That was better than him turning green before me when he gasped at the urgent care. Every time I'd have flashback memories of what he looked like, it felt like my intestines would knot. Later, I asked God to erase that memory from my brain. It was too painful for me to remember.

Most of the guests at the funeral home that day went to see

my son's corpse. Loved ones came from everywhere to support us. Mama Beatrice came with her friends. Michael's and my friends and family from Texas, Louisiana, and Florida as well. My Pastor, Ron Watty, and his wife, Tyra Watty – with whom I developed a close relationship, she was like my spiritual mommy – came to support us, represent New Life Church, and deliver the sermon for the funeral service, too.

A couple of weeks before the funeral, I asked God what I'd talk about in my eulogy. The Holy Spirit led me to Joshua 1:9, which was the scripture He gave me when I was moving from Cameroon to the US. So, when they called me out to give my eulogy, I preached. I remembered talking more about Jesus than I did about Caleb. I invited my audience to seek God and build a relationship with Him. I talked about my strength, which was from God and not myself. By myself, I would never have been able to make it. Then I concluded by telling my friends and family that if they desired to see Caleb one day again, they needed to give their lives to Christ because that's who Caleb was with. And when I was done, I went back to my seat near Michael, and they played 'The Goodness of God' by Bethel Music. I couldn't help it. I sobbed out loud bitterly as Tyra held me as if she was sheltering me in her arms, like the loving mommy she was to me. It was final – I would never see my son again in this life.

Then, it was Jessica's turn to read her eulogy. I knew no one better than her could talk about Caleb the way I expected her to. Apart from Michael and myself, no one really experienced life with Caleb both in Cameroon and the US like Jessica did. Her eulogy read:

Baby,

Where do I start? It's been such a short yet beautiful journey to have you in our lives…. 20 years ago, your mum became my friend, and the years went by to make her my sister. Later, she brought Mike to us, and then together they brought you…! YOU! CALEB TOBY PHILLIPS is an extraordinary spiral of happiness, joy, and love. You came into this world and made Corine a mother and Mike a father. You made Mummy Judy and Maman Albie's grandmothers; You made Papa Thobie and Uncle Tom grandfathers. You made Love, Ornella, Fabiola, and I aunties, and of course Patrick, Cedric, Dany, Manu, and Brian uncles! "Tchoutchou" as we will all call you, but "Bae" as I will most particularly call you…! Can I exaggerate to say that you are the cutest child in our lives to this day? Our sunshine and bundle of grace.

Ooooohhh yes, we cry for you, yes, we miss you, and yes, we do not understand why you went so young… but in GOD we pour our sorrow, in GOD we rest our hearts, and in GOD we put our faith…cuz truth is, we all belong to HIM.

When your mummy was pregnant, I remember telling her how much I wanted you to be a girl, and when you were born, for a second, I got scared; I don't even know why,… but then, later, I came back to carry you again, and a giant overflow of love arose in my heart like no other one before… to tell me that GOD made you perfect; little but mighty, bright and cheerful, kind and loving, adorable and polite, a funny player, and a happy little being, quick to say a funny "no" even when you wanted to say yes! (Lol). It feels to me that you grew sooooo fast, baby, and now you are gone so soon, too… Leaving us with the best memories and lessons of love. Thanks to you, we came to know Mike as the most amazing, caring, and loving father ever. And Corine is the superwoman version of a mother and wife. Your parents are probably the best thing that GOD could ever give to you cuz I can tell you, they loved you to the moon, until after the moon, and back here, over and over again.

Baby-mine, as a ceaseless whisper in my heart, let me tell you again, "I LOVE YOU". Today, amid my pain, I am happy that I was a giant part of your life and that even when I failed to be a perfect godmother, our love bond stood so great that no one could ever come close...

I can't find the words to console anyone here cuz actually, I wish we were not here. I want to sing "Let It Shine" and watch "Paw Patrol" with you. I want to bite your banana and drink juice from the small cup you used to hold with your little hands... I want to sleep on your bed with you... I want to hear you talk to me with energy in your childish language I do not understand... I want to laugh at your dance moves on country music and melt to your heartwarming "pleeaasseee mummy". Cuz I don't want you to go, but yet... you are gone; gone to GOD!

Singing "Oceans – HILLSONG UNITED"

Spirit lead me where my trust is without borders

Let me walk upon the waters

Wherever You would call me

Take me deeper than my feet could ever wander

And my faith will be made stronger

In the presence of my Savior

Following her speech, 'Oceans' by Hillsong United was performed. It was such an emotionally heavy moment, but I thanked God for His presence that day. We all met after the service at Aunt Lynette's house (Michael's aunt) and shared a meal. The following day, on our way to Houston, Michael, Jessica, and I stopped by the graveyard to see where Caleb was buried. Sometimes, I think about it and wonder how I'd have been able to handle this weekend if Jessica hadn't made it to the US to keep me grounded.

Life on earth is not all there is. This can be good news for some and bad news for others, but the reality remains that life on Earth is not all there is. There is life after death.

When I was a child, I used to think that Christmas was the most important Christian celebration, but as I grew up in faith, I came to realize that for me, Easter is where the level of the game changed. If Jesus, after the three days in the tomb, didn't resurrect, Christianity would make no sense. Jesus' ministry wouldn't be complete. It is through His resurrection that we know He had victory over death.

The moment I started understanding that if Jesus is alive, then it was possible that my son too wasn't dead, my deep sorrow gradually dissipated, and I was able to believe and say out loud that "my son is not dead." I've heard people saying that I was in denial, but I want to make this clear: I have never refuted Caleb's departure. I knew he was gone. I wished and even dreamed a couple of times that I was saving him from different accidents. I've been in extreme shock, thinking that he'd come back from daycare and hug me, but never did I create an imaginary life where my boy was still alive on this earth. Perhaps all of this was my denial phase, but I didn't stay in that phase too long not to accept that my son was gone.

I'm grateful today that my mom did an amazing job at teaching my siblings and me God's ways. So, when Caleb passed, I knew he went to heaven because my mom told me when I was younger that children don't go to hell (a place where powers of evil and terror reign, away from the presence of God). They go to heaven because they didn't reach the level of maturity where they knew right from wrong well enough to be judged like adults. That's why, she added, by your teenage years, you're big enough to know right from wrong and decide to follow God or not and bear the consequences of your choice.

He will wipe every tear from their eyes. There will be no more death or mourning or crying or pain, for the old order of things has passed away. Revelation 21:4 [NIV]

This is a promise he made us. Today, when I think about my son, tears of joy flow down my cheeks. My son is in a safe place where I don't have to worry about him. When my time comes to leave this earth, I will see Caleb again. And that will be a joyful moment for my soul. We will laugh, play, dance, and cuddle again. I've thought a couple of times what I will jokingly tell him, "Dude, you really left me down there, huh?" And I've imagined how he'd laugh, hold me tight, and tell me he loves me and he missed me too. I'm looking forward to that day. It's the hope I hold onto. And that gives me joy and peace like no one can imagine. Caleb, my happy kid, is in a happy place.

Today, I can talk about my death without fear in my spirit because I know where I'm going and who I'll meet, but I know I still have a lot to accomplish, and no premature death will take me away. I'm grateful for how Caleb's departure has made heaven real to me. Now, I can embrace the concept of eternity and hold onto it because I never want to be separated from the people I love. I want to do heaven with every single one of them.

I'm grateful that I never grieved like an unbeliever who is in a dark and hopeless place to be when they've lost a loved one. I've seen my husband grieve with such deep and dark sorrow because he saw no hope of ever seeing his son again. But like I told him, it's only in Jesus that you'll ever be able to grieve differently. Dead is not the end of Caleb. It is the beginning of eternity, and again, only with Jesus can you partake in this joyful hope. There are days I still bitterly grieve, but that's because I genuinely miss Caleb. Like any parent, I'd have wished to celebrate his birthdays and all major events of his life here, but I'm reminded constantly that it is nothing compared to the eternal life we'll celebrate together in heaven.

As if losing my son wasn't enough, one year after that, in May 2020, I lost my aunt Jeanine. She was the firstborn from my mom's side, kind of our matriarch. Some of her daughters and I were more than just cousins; we were very good friends, and I remembered telling one of them when I had her over the phone the day after the news was broken down to me, "Hold on firm to your faith, it will help you during this tragic season".

My son Caleb would have been four years old on June 27, 2020, and though sometimes I still felt like it was a dream and someone would wake me up from it, I knew deep down this was real; he was gone to be with Jesus.

"You're so strong". "I don't know how you do this". These are some of the words people told me when I just lost Caleb. At the moment, I had no idea where my strength was coming from. All I knew was that He is close to the brokenhearted [Psalm 34:18]. I believed it, and whenever I felt deep sorrow, I screamed it out to Him: "You said You were close to people like me; why can't I feel it? This is just too hard". And every single time the pain was that deep, I had someone showing up for me on the phone with either scripture or just a listening ear. It happened in total six times! Don't get me wrong, I was sad all day, every day, in tears all day, every day, but only six times did it happen that my pain was so deep I thought I'd die in my pool of tears with a crushed heart.

About two days after Caleb left, I had Ornella and Jessica on a video call from Cameroon. I danced and praised God with a popular church song from home. I encouraged them to dance with me. My mom and my aunt, Huguette, were with them, watching at the back of the call. Where did I find the strength to cheer them up and encourage them to be strong when I was the one who had just lost my only son? One thing I knew and rejoiced about was the fact that my son was in a better place, saved from the aches of this world. When His word said that death has no more power because of His Son's sacrifice [1 Corinthians 15:55-57] and one day we'll get to meet and rejoice again [John 16:22], I believed it!

"Not every thought in your mind comes from you." I've been taught about it time and again in Church. Going through an event that traumatic, I had no idea how loud the voice of the enemy would be amplified in my mind. Neither did I expect it to shake me to the point of coming close to losing my faith. "If God loved you, He wouldn't have taken away your son. Plus, does the Bible not say that He can resurrect people from the dead? With all the prayers in tongues you did that day, why didn't He save your son?" The more I heard those, the more I started doubting. It went on and on for some time then I realized this couldn't happen to me! I couldn't afford to lose the only thing that kept me going - my relationship with Him, especially not after losing the most important human being in my life.

Though my soul was diving into the deepest darkness, something in me knew that I couldn't survive without my faith. So, I managed to utter a simple prayer: "Lord, I can't afford to lose our relationship, though I'm finding no interest in it anymore. Save me!", and then I cried bitterly, as expressed in Psalm 18:6. Thankfully, I had the support of my spiritual leaders, friends, and family praying for me, which was immensely helpful. The doubting voices returned occasionally, but my approach to them had shifted. I constantly reminded myself of His perfect love for me and my family.

I didn't endure the most difficult first months of grieving because of my strength. Rather, it was the strength of God within me, manifesting in my weakest moments. My faith may not have always been steadfast, but God's stance towards me remained unchanged. He continued to love me through my doubts and grief. I understood one crucial thing: for a loving God to perform His miraculous work, a willing heart is needed, and I was fully willing. My faith, for which He is both the author and perfecter, indeed saved me.

PHOTO ALBUM

My dear Caleb, when you entered this world, you transformed us. You may not have lived very long, but your impact on our lives and the lives of those around you was immeasurable. I am thankful for all that we shared, and I wish I could have one more hug, or one more birthday party, or one more celebration of everything. Thankfully, I have an entire gallery of memories that remind me of what a precious child you were. I love you so much.

"I asked the Lord to give me this boy, and he has granted my request.
Now I am giving him to the Lord, and he will belong to the Lord his
whole life." 1 Samuel 1:27-28

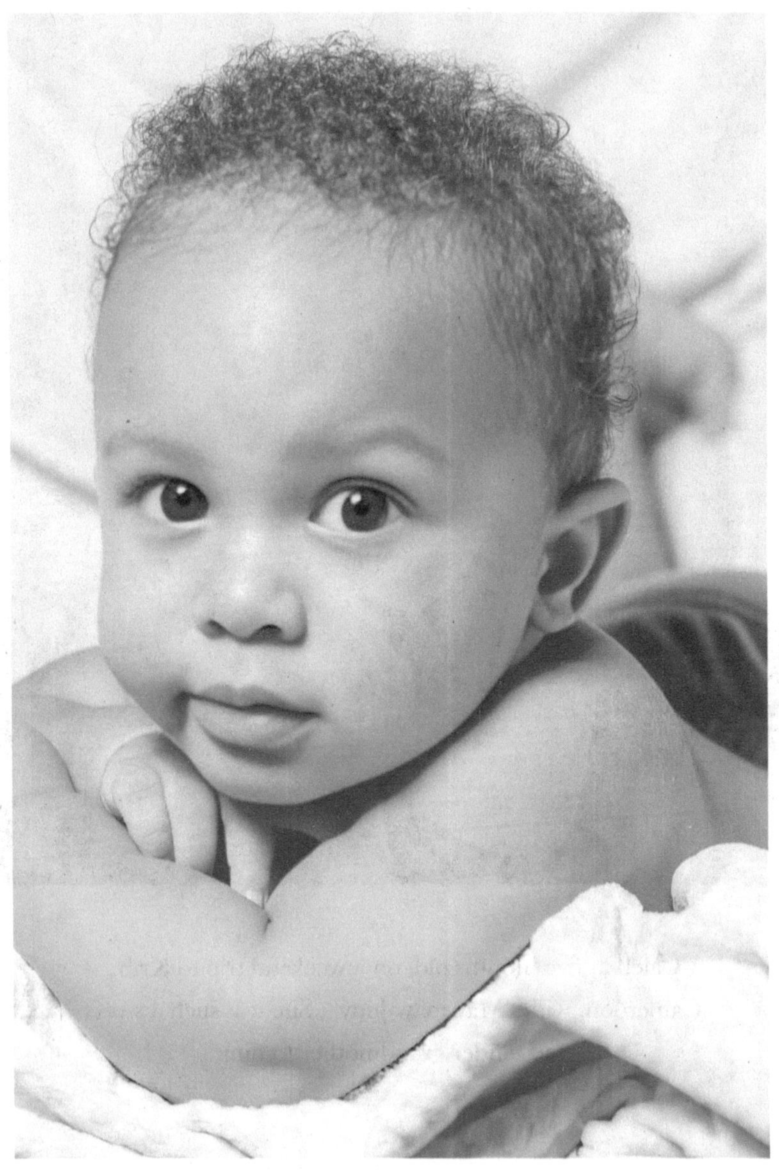

I look into Caleb's eyes and all I can see is the beauty of
his soul. How could something so perfect come out of me,
I still don't have an answer.

Caleb at five months old, on a weekend trip to Kribi, Cameroon, with "Mawmaw Judy". She was such a sweet and tender grandmother to him.

At Caleb's dedication party, with my siblings and cousins.
From left to right, Isabelle, Danilo (Caleb's godfather),
Yanelle, Brian, Myself, Caleb, Yolissa, Love (Caleb's
godmother), and Manu.

"These two right here, they are my blessing. They are my
miracle" Michael said of us during his speech at Caleb's
first birthday party. I loved who we were together.

My mom, "Mamie Albie" and her "Trecy" – understand,
her treasure – like she used to affectionately call him. I
always knew she loved my son more than she loved me,
but isn't that what grandparents do?

Holding hands and looking in the same direction. The connection between my son and my dad was one that always melted my heart. Caleb's middle name, Toby, was a way for us to honor my dad, Thobie.

Bath time was his favorite time. No matter how long he'd
stay in the tub, he was always unhappy when we got him
out of the water.

Meeting Michael's family for the first time during
Thanksgiving 2017 at Aunt Lynette's house. From left to
right, Mawmaw Judy, Caleb, Cruze, Willow, Amy, Mia,
and Aunt Dollie.

On our wedding day. During the entire ceremony, Caleb won't leave us. He stood there by us through the exchange of our rings, vows, and prayers. He was the glue that held us together.

I'll forever be the only girl he exchanged a kiss with. How
I wished one day I could have walked him down the aisle
on his wedding day. Nonetheless, I'm grateful he witnessed
my union with his dad.

That night when he silently made a sleeping nest in
my back, while I was studying for my interior design
course. At such a young age, Caleb was so thoughtful and
emotionally aware.

Caleb, our happy kid, on his second birthday at the
daycare. He had such a fun time celebrating with his
friends. We never got to celebrate his third birthday. I
think about it sometimes, and it still hurts so bad.

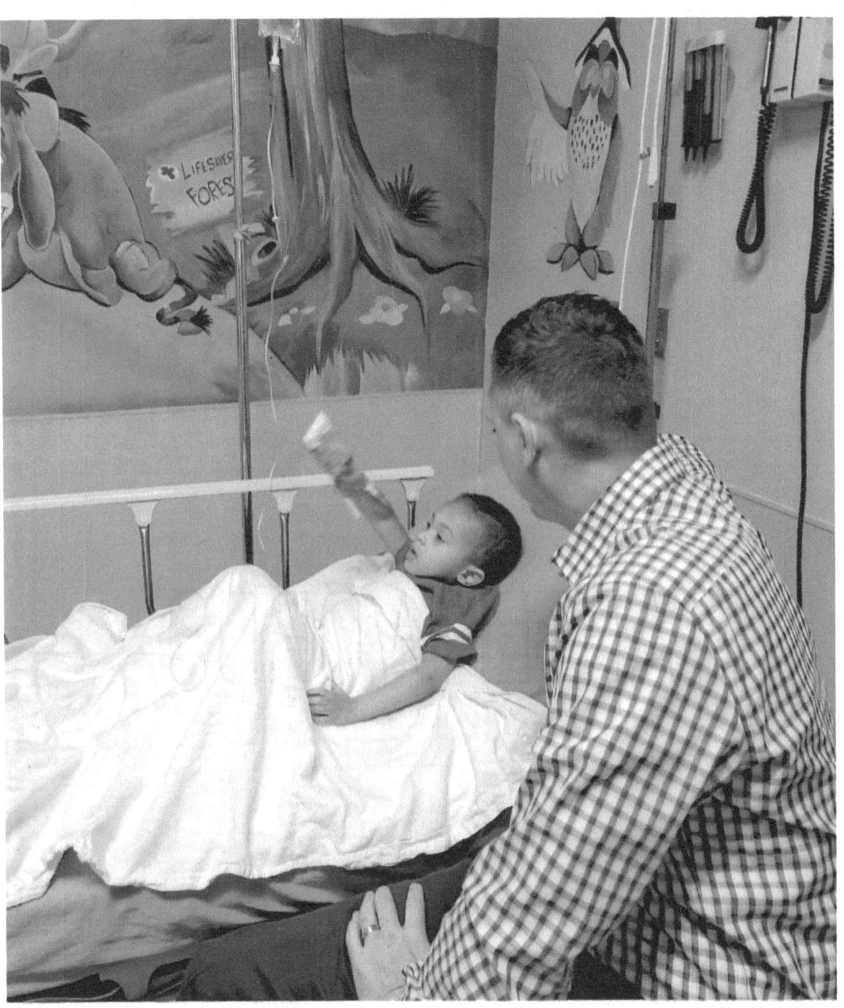

Monday, March 11, 2019. It is in this bed that my son passed away. Nothing pointed to the fact that this would be our last moment with him. There he was, watching cartoons with his Papa for the last time. We miss you, son.

4
AFTERWORDS

When the Lord gave me the task of writing this book, I delayed for about two years to obey. I didn't know how I'd do it nor where I'd find the strength to do so. I went through doubts, discouragement, and even a broken marriage during this time. I almost gave up on ever writing this book. Like Paulo Coelho said, "Tears are words that need to be written." I wrote because I needed Caleb to be remembered. I wrote because I needed my story to be heard. I wrote because I needed to obey God, no matter my circumstances. I wrote because I wanted to share my journey of grief and who God was to me during these years.

Following Caleb's departure, my relationship with Michael seemed to be stable for a full year, but very quickly, it faced the same difficulties we'd been struggling with for years. I broke up with him and was adamant about never going back with him. But God had a different plan for us. After a year and a half apart, we reunited. Today, our marriage is the healthiest it's ever been. God restored us individually during our breakup and provided a better foundation for our relationship. We're still a work in progress, but I know that what God starts, he will finish. I'm now waiting for the day my husband will confess Christ as his Lord and Savior, and that day will surely come to pass. It is a promise the Lord made to me, and I hold on firmly to it. As for me and my house, we will serve the Lord and my husband will take his position and role of spiritual leader in this family.

And because a blessing never comes alone, the Lord blessed us with a precious little girl, Zélie. She was born prematurely on March 31, 2023, but that wasn't an incident. God is so intentional that I believe He allowed it to happen exactly that way. She came into this world the same month Caleb passed away. If this isn't a wink from God, then I do not know what it is. I bless Him for the health of our daughter. I look at her, and I wonder how I could have lived this life without this little human being. Her beauty takes my breath away, and I'm in the front row, watching how God will mature her into the woman he destined her to be. Through her, He wiped away our tears and gave us hope for the future again.

Sometime around October 2020, I launched my interior design business after getting my diploma the year before that. My son might not be around to cheer me up, but I'm doing my best to honor his memory by pushing harder every day with this company. There are times it is tougher than other days, times when I want to abandon this dream, but I believe that God, who made it possible so far, will see it through. At the back of my mind, I will always remember and cherish that night Caleb made his bed and slept behind me in the kitchen while I was studying.

Caleb's death didn't come to break my faith. Through it, God built strength and resilience in me. Over the past five years following his death, my story has encouraged and inspired some people. When I was going through fire, I couldn't see past my pain. Each day was a struggle. Today, I witness how my compassion and understanding of people has matured. I never want to go through this again, and I hold tightly on God's promise of never letting shame knock at my door again.

Sharing my story of grief doesn't mean I don't cry anymore. I do and probably will till I die. I live every day with this hole in my heart, yet I know that God's love for me is unshakeable. It passes through pain, healing every wound. I will still cry, but I know I'm not alone. I have the assurance that my Lord Jesus walks this walk of faith by my side every single day.

May you find peace in your grieving journey, and may the love of our savior be revealed to you in the hope that you'd embrace it. Be blessed.

ACKNOWLEDGMENTS

I want to give a special thanks to:

Abba, My Father; Jesus, My Savior; and the Holy Spirit, my best friend, for showing me love as I went through the fire. Each one of you – though all the same – showed up for me in a specific way. I'm grateful to be known and loved by you.

Martha Guiala, for years now, you have been my spiritual partner and one of my fierce prayer supporters. When I am weak, you're there to strengthen me. Thank you for encouraging me to write this book, and reminding me that obeying God about this assignment was the most important thing in my walk with Him. Your friendship means the world to me.

My husband, Michael Phillips, for existing. I read somewhere that the fires of refinement come with a cost, but also with a promise. It hasn't always been easy but I look back today at our story and I realize it was all worth it. I'm a better woman and believer because of what I went through with you. You have always been God's choice for me. It just took me longer to realize it. With all my heart, I love you.

My son, Caleb Phillips, for bringing love and joy around you. I miss your many facial expressions, your cuddles, and your "please moh-meee". I know you are in a better place, and I can't wait to meet you there when my time comes. What a day of celebration it will be!

My parents, Thobie and Albertine Essama, for not only praying and encouraging me from afar but for being amazing grandparents to Caleb. Mom, I can't be thankful enough for the impact you've had on my spiritual life. You showed me Jesus, and when my time came, I embraced Him and never looked back. Dad, thank you for always giving me the freedom to express myself and speak my mind. I'm able to courageously follow my dreams because of how you've always validated me. You're the coolest dad I know.

My husband's mom and stepfather, Judy and Tom Seay, for being such caring and loving grandparents to Caleb. Mommy Judy, I know how hard it was for you to bury another Caleb – your youngest son, then your grandson. I know you think sometimes that life is unfair, and it sure is. But in the midst of it, I hope you'll keep holding onto God's peace. You're blessed to have a husband like yours who supports and loves you.

Aunt Dollie and Uncle Tony Mayeux, for being our parents' figure in Houston from the moment we moved to this country to when Caleb left. At your house, I had my dream wedding. At your house, I had my toughest week after Caleb's departure. All of these matter so much to me and I will forever be grateful for opening the doors to your house to us.

My siblings and their partners, Patrick and Natasha, Cedric, Danilo and Yanelle, Love, and Brian for being the best uncles and aunties Caleb could have asked for. Pat and Tash, you did not meet him in person, yet I saw how much you loved him dearly from afar. Your dedication towards Caleb was remarkable. I made you, Love, and Danilo, his godparents because I knew I could trust his spiritual upbringing into your hands. Cedric, Thanksgiving with you in Florida will always be one of my most cherished memories of seeing Caleb and you bonding together. What did I do to deserve such love from you Brian, I do not know. Thank you for extending it to my son. I know how much you miss him.

The Kpanda and The Mbome family (my dad and mom's extended family respectively) back home in Cameroon and around the world for constantly checking on us as we were going through this tragedy. I know that if you could, you would have made it to assist me during the funeral. Nonetheless, I felt your presence from afar. Thank you for all the prayers and the calls. I'm grateful to be part of both your clans.

The Phillips and The Anselme family, for your relentless love, support, and acceptance of Michael, Caleb, and I, just as we were. You made me feel welcome and that in itself is a precious gift. I'm grateful I had you to organize the entire funeral. I will forever cherish the memories of Thanksgiving in Holmwood, Easter in Anacoco, and everything in between. You are priceless to me.

Ornella Kamga, Jessica Nang, Fabiola Nguetsop, Myriam N'dri, Corine Tsimi, and Odette Leukouo, for your friendship. From my pregnancy till Caleb's death, you have been so present in our lives. They say it takes a village to raise a child. You were my village, my friends. Thank you for considering him as one of yours. How blessed he was to have you all as his "aunty-mommies".

Pastor Mary Kemp-Smith, Mrs. Tyra Watty, and the entire New Life Church family for letting me cry in your arms and ask you strange questions about death and heaven. I'm not sure I'd have been able to make it if I didn't have you guys. All the comfort, counseling, and prayers you brought to my soul were priceless. Thank you for being my other family.

My friends from Horizon Bilingual Educational Complex and St Francis College; My friends from Faculty of Industrial Engineering; My friends from Bethel World Outreach Ministries (now Harvest

Intercontinental Ministries); My Cameroonian community and friends from Houston; My community from Instagram; My husband's best friends and Tiger Droppings community for putting your resources, be it financially, emotionally or spiritually together, to show us how much you cared.

ABOUT THE AUTHOR

Corine E. Phillips, a resilient soul born and raised in the vibrant landscapes of Cameroon, now calls the USA her home. A devoted wife and a loving mother, Corine's journey through grief has inspired her to pen down her book, "When I Lost My Son to Him," an emotional exploration of love, loss, and the unwavering strength found in surrendering to the will of God.

In her role as a mother, Corine faced the heart-wrenching loss of her 2-year-old son, Caleb. Through her words, she extends a compassionate hand to parents going through grief, offering comfort and guidance. However, Corine's message surpasses worldly boundaries, resonating with anyone who has felt the weight of loss.

In "When I Lost My Son to Him," Corine seeks to convey a powerful message rooted in faith and surrender. Through her intimate narrative, she emphasizes the importance of trusting God, highlighting that true surrender is borne out of a deep knowledge of His character. Amid life's darkest moments, Corine's story reminds us that God is ever-present, offering protection and solace to the broken-hearted.

Despite this being her inaugural project into the literary world, Corine's lifelong dream of becoming an author has been a driving force in her life. A natural storyteller, she previously boarded on an investigative writing endeavor during her teenage years, though the manuscript was regrettably lost before completion.

Beyond her literary pursuits, Corine is a multi-talented individual with a background in Safety Engineering, having graduated a decade ago. Moreover, she is a creative force as an Interior Designer, working and managing her own design business.

Her interests extend to journaling, decorating, designing, and sharing insights on fashion, faith, and lifestyle through her engaging Instagram platform.

Corine's authenticity shines through in her role as a helper and confidante. Her ability to transform the ordinary into the beautiful, coupled with her thorough and organized nature, has earned her a lot of praise. She is a patient and good listener, a quality that is rare to find now. Determined, uplifting, and unconventional, Corine E. Phillips is not just an author; she is a beacon of hope and a testament to the resilience of the human spirit. Her journey from grief to grace is an inspiration to all who seek comfort in the embrace of faith. Find out more about Corine E. Phillips on her Instagram page.